W9-CBB-967

BUSINESS

SECOND EDITION

Ferguson
An imprint of ☑ Facts On File

Careers in Focus: Business, Second Edition

Copyright © 2005 by Facts On File, Inc.

Ferguson
An imprint of Facts On File, Inc.
132 West 31st Street
New York NY 10001

Library of Congress Cataloging-in-Publication Data

Careers in focus. Business.— 2nd ed.
  p. cm.
  Includes bibliographical references and index.
  ISBN 0-8160-5864-4 (hardcover : alk. paper)
  1. Business—Vocational guidance—Juvenile literature. [1. Business—Vocational guidance. 2. Vocational guidance.] I. J.G. Ferguson Publishing Company.
  HF5381.2.C375 2005
  331.702—dc22   2004007140

Ferguson books are available at special discounts when purchased in bulk quantities for businesses, associations, institutions, or sales promotions. Please call our Special Sales Department in New York at (212) 967-8800 or (800) 322-8755.

You can find Ferguson on the World Wide Web at http://www.fergpubco.com

Text design by David Strelecky

Printed in the United States of America

MP JT 10 9 8 7 6 5 4 3 2 1

This book is printed on acid-free paper.

Table of Contents

Introduction 1

Accountants and Auditors 4

Billing Clerks 17

Bookkeeping and Accounting Clerks 23

Business Managers 29

Cultural Advisers 40

Customer Service Representatives 47

Data Entry Clerks 56

Event Planners 63

Executive Recruiters 73

Labor Union Business Agents 81

Management Analysts and Consultants 89

Office Administrators 97

Office Clerks 104

Personnel and Labor Relations Specialists . . . 111

Public Relations Specialists 125

Purchasing Agents 133

Receptionists 141

Secretaries 148

Stock Clerks 157

Temporary Workers 164

Typists and Word Processors 173

Index 181

Introduction

All businesses can be defined as organizations that provide customers with the goods and services they want. There are three main types of businesses in the U.S. economy: manufacturers, merchandisers, and service providers. From skateboards to limousines, virtually everything around you comes from a manufacturing firm of some sort. Merchandisers are businesses that help move products through a channel of distribution to the consumer or end-user. Service providers are businesses that do not sell an actual product but perform a service for a fee. Common examples of service providers are restaurants, dry cleaners, hotels, and hair stylists.

Although there is a wide variety of corporate structures, almost every successful company's structure requires a core group of employees in the area of production, marketing, finance, human resources, and support services. Production includes conceptualizing, designing, and creating products and services. Marketing is the process of distributing and promoting the company's product to the right people at the right time. Finance involves the management of a company's money. Human resources or personnel management deals with all aspects of a company's employee culture, including recruiting, hiring, training, evaluating, disciplining, administering benefits, and resolving conflicts. Support services maintain a company's internal workings, including recordkeeping, secretarial, and management services.

Because it is such a broad category, it is difficult to project growth for business as a whole. While some industries thrive, others decline. There are certain trends, however, that affect business as a whole. For example, all businesses are affected by changes in the economy. When the economy is thriving, consumers have more money to spend, which means they buy more products and services. When the economy suffers a downturn, many businesses suffer as consumers cut back on spending. During tough economic times, many companies downsize and lay off employees in order to stay afloat.

Advances in and increased use of technology also affects all businesses. As industries become more automated, workers with technological know-how are becoming increasingly valuable. A downside of this trend is that as computers cut down on costs and the need for human work, some jobs may be eliminated or combined to reduce costs.

Each article in *Careers in Focus: Business* discusses a particular business occupation in detail. The articles appear in Ferguson's *Encyclopedia of Careers and Vocational Guidance* but have been updated and revised with the latest information from the U.S. Department of Labor and other sources.

The **Quick Facts** section provides a brief summary of the career including recommended school subjects, personal skills, work environment, minimum educational requirements, salary ranges, certification or licensing requirements, and employment outlook. This section also provides acronyms and identification numbers for the following government classification indexes: the *Dictionary of Occupational Titles* (DOT), the *Guide for Occupational Exploration* (GOE), the National Occupational Classification (NOC) index, and the Occupational Information Network (O*NET)-Standard Occupational Classification System (SOC) index. The DOT, GOE, and O*NET-SOC indexes have been created by the U.S. government; the NOC index is Canada's career classification system. Readers can use the identification numbers listed in the Quick Facts section to access further information on a career. Print editions of the DOT (*Dictionary of Occupational Titles.* Indianapolis, Ind.: JIST Works, 1991) and GOE (*The Complete Guide for Occupational Exploration.* Indianapolis, Ind.: JIST Works, 1993) are available at libraries, and electronic versions of the NOC (http://www23.hrdc-drhc.gc.ca/2001/e/generic/welcome.shtml) and O*NET-SOC (http://online.onetcenter.org) are available on the World Wide Web. When no DOT, GOE, NOC, or O*NET-SOC numbers are present, this means that the U.S. Department of Labor or the Human Resources Development Canada have not created a numerical designation for this career. In this instance, you will see the acronym "N/A," or not available.

The **Overview** section is a brief introductory description of the duties and responsibilities of someone in the career. Oftentimes, a career may have a variety of job titles. When this is the case, alternative career titles are presented in this section.

The **History** section describes the history of the particular career as it relates to the overall development of its industry or field.

The Job describes the primary and secondary duties of the career.

Requirements discusses high school and postsecondary education and training requirements, any certification or licensing necessary, and any other personal requirements for success in the career.

Exploring offers suggestions on how to gain some experience in or knowledge of the particular job before making a firm educational and financial commitment. The focus is on what can be done while still in high school (or in the early years of college) to gain a better understanding of the career.

The **Employers** section gives an overview of typical places of employment for the job.

Starting Out discusses the best ways to land that first job, be it through the college placement office, newspaper ads, or personal contacts.

The **Advancement** section describes what kind of career path to expect from the career and how to get on it.

Earnings lists salary ranges and describes the typical fringe benefits.

The **Work Environment** section describes the typical surroundings and conditions of employment—whether indoors or outdoors, noisy or quiet, social or independent, and so on. Also discussed are typical hours worked, any seasonal fluctuations, and the stresses and strains of the job.

The **Outlook** section summarizes the career in terms of the general economy and industry projections. For the most part, Outlook information is obtained from the Bureau of Labor Statistics and is supplemented by information taken from professional associations. Job growth terms follow those used in the *Occupational Outlook Handbook*. Growth described as "much faster than the average" means an increase of 36 percent or more. Growth described as "faster than the average" means an increase of 21–35 percent. Growth described as "about as fast as the average" means an increase of 10–20 percent. Growth described as "more slowly than the average" means an increase of 3–9 percent. Growth described as "little or no change" means an increase of 0–2 percent. "Decline" means a decrease of 1 percent or more.

Each article ends with **For More Information,** which lists organizations that can provide career information on training, education, internships, scholarships, and job placement.

As you explore the wide variety of careers in business that are presented in this book, consider which of them might best suit your personality, strengths, and general career goals. Be sure to contact the organizations listed at the end of each article for more information.

Accountants and Auditors

QUICK FACTS

School Subjects
Business
Economics

Personal Skills
Following instructions
Leadership/management

Work Environment
Primarily indoors
One location with some travel

Minimum Education Level
Bachelor's degree

Salary Range
$23,442 to $51,070 to
$197,500+

Certification or Licensing
Recommended

Outlook
About as fast as the average

DOT
160

GOE
11.06.01

NOC
1111

O*NET-SOC
13-2011.00, 13-2011.01,
13-2011.02

OVERVIEW

Accountants compile, analyze, verify, and prepare financial records, including profit and loss statements, balance sheets, cost studies, and tax reports. Accountants may specialize in areas such as auditing, tax work, cost accounting, budgeting and control, or systems and procedures. Accountants also may specialize in a particular business or field; for example, *agricultural accountants* specialize in drawing up and analyzing financial statements for farmers and for farm equipment companies. *Auditors* examine and verify financial records to ensure that they are accurate, complete, and in compliance with federal laws. There are approximately 1.1 million accountants and auditors employed in the United States.

HISTORY

Accounting records and bookkeeping methods have been used from early history to the present. Records discovered in Babylonia (modern-day Iraq) date back to 3600 B.C., and accounts were kept by the Greeks and the Romans.

Modern accounting began with the technique of double-entry bookkeeping, which was developed in the 15th and 16th centuries by Luca Pacioli, an Italian mathematician. After the industrial revolution, business grew more complex. As government and industrial institutions developed in the 19th and 20th centuries, accurate records and information were needed to assist in making decisions on economic and management policies.

The accounting profession in the United States dates back only to 1880, when English and Scottish investors began buying stock in American companies. To keep an eye on their investments, they sent accountants to the United States who realized the great potential that existed in the accounting field and stayed on to establish their own businesses.

Federal legislation, such as the income tax in 1913 and the excess profits tax in 1917, helped cause an accounting boom that has made the profession instrumental to all business.

Accountants have long been considered "bean counters," and their work has been written off by outsiders as routine and boring. However, their image, once associated with death, taxes, and bad news, is making a turnaround. Accountants now do much more than prepare financial statements and record business transactions. Technology now counts the "beans," allowing accountants to analyze and interpret the results. Their work has expanded to encompass challenging and creative tasks such as computing costs and efficiency gains of new technologies, participating in strategies for mergers and acquisitions, supervising quality management, and designing and using information systems to track financial performance.

THE JOB

Accountants' duties depend on the size and nature of the company in which they are employed. The major fields of employment are public, private, and government accounting.

Public accountants work independently on a fee basis or as members of an accounting firm, and they perform a variety of tasks for businesses or individuals. These may include auditing accounts and records, preparing and certifying financial statements, conducting financial investigations and furnishing testimony in legal matters, and assisting in formulating budget policies and procedures.

Private accountants, sometimes called *industrial* or *management accountants,* handle financial records of the firms at which they are employed.

Government accountants work on the financial records of government agencies or, when necessary, they audit the records of private companies. In the federal government, many accountants are employed as *bank examiners, Internal Revenue Service agents,* and *investigators,* as well as in regular accounting positions.

Within these fields, accountants can specialize in a variety of areas.

General accountants supervise, install, and devise general accounting, budget, and cost systems. They maintain records, balance books, and prepare and analyze statements on all financial aspects of business. Administrative officers use this information to make sound business decisions.

Budget accountants review expenditures of departments within a firm to make sure expenses allotted are not exceeded. They also aid in drafting budgets and may devise and install budget-control systems.

Cost accountants determine unit costs of products or services by analyzing records and depreciation data. They classify and record all operating costs so that management can control expenditures.

Property accountants keep records of equipment, buildings, and other property owned or leased by a company. They prepare mortgage schedules and payments as well as appreciation or depreciation statements, which are used for income tax purposes.

Environmental accountants help utilities, manufacturers, and chemical companies set up preventive systems to ensure environmental compliance and provide assistance in the event that legal issues arise.

Systems accountants design and set up special accounting systems for organizations whose needs cannot be handled by standardized procedures. This may involve installing automated or computerized accounting processes and includes instructing personnel in the new methods.

Forensic accountants and auditors use accounting principles and theories to support or oppose claims being made in litigation.

Tax accountants prepare federal, state, or local tax returns of an individual, business, or corporation according to prescribed rates, laws, and regulations. They also may conduct research on the effects of taxes on firm operations and recommend changes to reduce taxes. This is one of the most intricate fields of accounting, and many accountants therefore specialize in one particular phase such as corporate, individual income, or property tax.

Assurance accountants help improve the quality of information for clients in assurance services areas such as electronic commerce, risk assessment, and elder care. This information may be financial or nonfinancial in nature.

Auditors ensure that financial records are accurate, complete, and in compliance with federal laws. To do so they review items in original entry books, including purchase orders, tax returns, billing statements, and other important documents. Auditors may also prepare financial statements for clients and suggest ways to improve productivity and profits. *Internal auditors* conduct the same kind of examination and evaluation for one particular company. Because they are salaried employees of that company, their financial audits must be certified by a qualified independent auditor. Internal auditors also review procedures and controls, appraise the efficiency and effectiveness of operations, and make sure their companies comply with corporate policies and government regulations.

Tax auditors review financial records and other information provided by taxpayers to determine the appropriate tax liability. State and federal tax auditors usually work in government offices, but they may perform a field audit in a taxpayer's home or office.

Revenue agents are employed by the federal government to examine selected income tax returns and, when necessary, conduct field audits and investigations to verify the information reported and adjust the tax liability accordingly.

Chief bank examiners enforce good banking practices throughout a state. They schedule bank examinations to ensure that financial institutions comply with state laws and, in certain cases, they take steps to protect a bank's solvency and the interests of its depositors and shareholders.

REQUIREMENTS

High School

If you are interested in an accounting career, you must be very proficient in arithmetic and basic algebra. Familiarity with computers and their applications is equally important. Course work in English and communications will also be beneficial.

Postsecondary Training

Postsecondary training in accounting may be obtained in a wide variety of institutions such as private business schools, junior colleges, universities, and correspondence schools. A bachelor's degree with a major in accounting, or a related field such as economics, is highly recommended by professional associations for those entering the field and is required by all states before taking the licensing exam. It is possible, however, to become a successful accountant by completing a program at any of the above-mentioned institutions. A four-year college curriculum usually includes about two years of liberal arts courses, a year of general business subjects, and a year of specific accounting work. Better positions, particularly in public accounting, require a bachelor's degree with a major in accounting. Large public accounting firms often prefer people with a master's degree in accounting. For beginning positions in accounting, the federal government requires four years of college (including 24 semester hours in accounting or auditing) or an equivalent combination of education and experience.

Certification or Licensing

Certified public accountants (CPAs) must pass a qualifying examination and hold a certificate issued by the state in which they wish to practice. In most states, a college degree is required for admission to the CPA examinations; a few states allow candidates to substitute years of public accounting experience for the college degree requirement. Currently 42 states and the District of Columbia require CPA candidates to have 150 hours of education, which is an additional 30 hours beyond the standard bachelor's degree. Five additional states plan to enact the 150-hour requirement in the future. These criteria can be met by combining an undergraduate accounting program with graduate study or participating in an integrated five-year professional accounting program. You can obtain information from a state board of accountancy or check out the website of the American Institute of Certified Public Accountants (AICPA) to read about new regulations and review last year's exam. (See the end of this article.)

The two-day Uniform CPA Examination administered by the AICPA is used by all states. Nearly all states require at least two years of public accounting experience or its equivalent before a CPA certificate can be earned.

Some accountants seek out other credentials. Those who have earned a bachelor's degree, pass a four-part examination, agree to meet continuing education requirements, and have at least two years of experience in management accounting may become a certified management accountant (CMA) through the Institute of Management Accounting.

The Accreditation Council for Accountancy and Taxation confers the following three designations: accredited business accountant (ABA), accredited tax preparer (ATP), and accredited tax advisor (ATA).

To become a certified internal auditor (CIA), college graduates with two years of experience in internal auditing must pass a four-part examination given by the Institute of Internal Auditors (IIA). The IIA also offers the following specialty certifications: certified financial services auditor and certified government auditing professional. Visit the IIA website for more information. (See the end of this article.)

The designation certified information systems auditor (CISA) is conferred by the Information Systems Audit and Control Association to candidates who pass an examination and who have five years of experience auditing electronic data-processing systems.

Other organizations, such as the Bank Administration Institute, confer specialized auditing designations.

Other Requirements

To be a successful accountant you will need strong mathematical, analytical, and problem-solving skills. You need to be able to think logically and to interpret facts and figures accurately. Effective oral and written communication skills are also essential in working with both clients and management.

Other important skills are attentiveness to detail, patience, and industriousness. Business acumen and the ability to generate clientele are crucial to service-oriented business, as are honesty, dedication, and a respect for the work of others.

EXPLORING

If you think a career as an accountant or auditor might be for you, try working in a retail business, either part time or during the summer. Working at the cash register or even pricing products as a stockperson is good introductory experience. You should also consider working as a treasurer for a student organization requiring financial planning and money management. It may be possible to gain some experience by volunteering with local groups such as churches and small businesses. You should also stay abreast of news in the field by reading trade magazines and checking out the industry websites of the AICPA and other accounting associations. The AICPA has numerous free educational publications available.

EMPLOYERS

Over 1 million people are employed as accountants and auditors. Accountants and auditors work throughout private industry and government. One out of five accountants and auditors work for accounting, auditing, and bookkeeping firms. Approximately 10 percent are self-employed. A large number of accountants and auditors are certified.

STARTING OUT

Junior public accountants usually start in jobs with routine duties such as counting cash, verifying calculations, and other detailed numerical work. In private accounting, beginners are likely to start as cost accountants and junior internal auditors. They may also enter in clerical positions as cost clerks, ledger clerks, and timekeepers or as trainees in technical or junior executive positions. In the federal government, most beginners are hired as trainees at the GS-5 level after passing the civil service exam.

Some state CPA societies arrange internships for accounting majors, and some offer scholarships and loan programs.

ADVANCEMENT

Talented accountants and auditors can advance quickly. Junior public accountants usually advance to senior positions within several years and to managerial positions soon after. Those successful in dealing with top-level management may eventually become supervisors, managers, and partners in larger firms or go into independent practice. However, only 2 to 3 percent of new hires advance to audit manager, tax manager, or partner.

Private accountants in firms may become audit managers, tax managers, cost accounting managers, or controllers, depending on their specialty. Some become controllers, treasurers, or corporation presidents. Others on the finance side may rise to become managers of financial planning and analysis or treasurers.

Federal government trainees are usually promoted within a year or two. Advancement to controller and to higher administrative positions is ultimately possible.

Although advancement may be rapid for skilled accountants, especially in public accounting, those with inadequate academic or professional training are often assigned to routine jobs and find it difficult to obtain promotions. All accountants find it necessary to continue their study of accounting and related areas in their spare time. Even those who have already obtained college degrees, gained experience, and earned a CPA certificate may spend many hours studying to keep up with new industry developments. Thousands of practicing accountants enroll in formal courses offered by universities and professional associations to specialize in certain areas of accounting, broaden or update their professional skills, and become eligible for advancement and promotion.

EARNINGS

According to the U.S. Department of Labor, beginning salaries for accountants with a bachelor's degree averaged $40,647 a year in 2003; those with a master's degree averaged $42,241 a year. Auditors with up to one year of experience earned between $29,500 and

$40,500, according to a 2003 survey by Robert Half International. Some experienced accountants and auditors may earn anywhere from $41,000 at the mid-level to $197,500 at the level of director. Salaries greatly depend on such factors as an applicant's education level, seniority, the size of the firm, and the firm's location.

Accountants and auditors working for the federal government generally make lower salaries than those who work in private industry or are self-employed. The average salary for accountants working for the federal government was $51,070 in 2003. The starting annual salary for junior accountants and auditors was $23,442. Candidates with superior academic records might start at $29,037, while applicants with a master's degree or two years of professional experience usually began at $35,519. Accountants employed by the federal government in nonsupervisory, supervisory, and managerial positions averaged $69,370 a year in 2003; auditors averaged $73,247.

Accountants in large firms and with large corporations receive typical benefits including paid vacation and sick days, insurance, and savings and pension plans. Employees in smaller companies generally receive fewer fringe benefits.

WORK ENVIRONMENT

Accounting is known as a desk job, and a 40-hour workweek can be expected in public and private accounting. Although computer work is replacing paperwork, the job can be routine and monotonous, and concentration and attention to detail are critical. Public accountants experience considerable pressure during the tax period, which runs from November to April, and they may have to work long hours. There is potential for stress aside from tax season, as accountants can be responsible for managing multimillion-dollar finances with no margin for error. Self-employed accountants and those working for a small firm can expect to work longer hours.

In smaller firms, most of the public accountant's work is performed in the client's office. A considerable amount of travel is often necessary to service a wide variety of businesses. In a larger firm, however, an accountant may have very little client contact, spending more time interacting with the accounting team.

OUTLOOK

In the wake of the massive changes that swept through the industry in the last decade, the job outlook for accountants and auditors is good, with employment expected to grow about as fast as the average through 2012, according to the U.S. Department of Labor.

Several factors will contribute to the expansion of the accounting industry: increasingly complex tax laws; economic growth, which will increase the size and the number of businesses required to release financial reports to stockholders; and increased scrutiny of accounting records in light of corporate scandals.

Recent federal legislation focuses have increased penalties for embezzlement, bribery, and securities fraud. As a result, there will be an increased demand for auditors and certified public accountants who can thoroughly audit businesses' financial records. There will also be an increased demand for forensic accountants to monitor financial transactions and detect financial crimes that occur over computer networks.

As firms specialize their services, accountants will need to follow suit. Firms will seek out accountants with experience in marketing and proficiency in computer systems to build management consulting practices. As trade and corporate outsourcing increase, so will the demand for CPAs with international specialties and foreign language skills. And CPAs with an engineering degree would be well equipped to specialize in environmental accounting. Other accounting specialties that will enjoy good prospects include assurance, forensic, and tax accounting.

While the majority of jobs will be found in large cities with large businesses, smaller firms will start up, and smaller businesses will continue to seek outside accountants. Accountants without college degrees will find more paraprofessional accounting positions, similar to the work of paralegals, as the number of lower- and mid-level workers expands. Demand will also be high for specialized accounting temps; CPA firms have started to hire temps to smooth out their staffing through seasonal business cycles.

The role of public accountants will change as they perform less auditing and tax work and assume greater management and consulting responsibilities. Likewise, private accountants will focus more on analyzing operations rather than simply providing data and will develop sophisticated accounting systems.

Accounting jobs are more secure than most during economic downswings. Despite fluctuations in the nation's economy, there will always be a need to manage financial information, especially as the number, size, and complexity of business transactions increases. However, competition for jobs will remain, certification requirements will become more rigorous, and accountants and auditors with the highest degrees will be the most competitive.

FOR MORE INFORMATION

For information on accreditation and testing, contact
Accreditation Council for Accountancy
and Taxation
1010 North Fairfax Street
Alexandria, VA 22314
Tel: 888-289-7763
Email: info@acatcredentials.org
http://www.acatcredentials.org

For information on the Uniform CPA Examination and student membership, contact
American Institute of Certified Public Accountants
1211 Avenue of the Americas
New York, NY 10036
Tel: 212-596-6200
http://www.aicpa.org

For information on accredited programs in accounting, contact
Association to Advance Collegiate
Schools of Business
600 Emerson Road, Suite 300
St. Louis, MO 63141
Tel: 314-872-8481
http://www.aacsb.edu

For information on certification for bank auditors, contact
Bank Administration Institute
One North Franklin, Suite 1000
Chicago, IL 60606-3421
Email: info@bai.org
Tel: 800-224-9889
http://www.bai.org

For more information on women in accounting, contact
Educational Foundation for
Women in Accounting
PO Box 1925
Southeastern, PA 19399
Tel: 610-407-9229
Email: info@efwa.org
http://www.efwa.org

For information on certification, contact
Information Systems Audit and Control Association
3701 Algonquin Road, Suite 1010
Rolling Meadows, IL 60008
Tel: 847-253-1545
Email: certification@isaca.org
http://www.isaca.org

For information on internal auditing and certification, contact
Institute of Internal Auditors
247 Maitland Avenue
Altamonte Springs, FL 32701
Tel: 407-937-1100
Email: iia@theiia.org
http://www.theiia.org

For information about management accounting and the CMA designation, as well as student membership, contact
Institute of Management Accountants
10 Paragon Drive
Montvale, NJ 07645
Tel: 800-638-4427
Email: ima@imanet.org
http://www.imanet.org

INTERVIEW

Claudio Guerrera is a senior staff accountant with Deloitte, a global provider of professional services, which include audit, tax, and consulting. Claudio spoke with the editors of Careers in Focus: Business *about his career.*

Q. What made you decide to become an accountant?
A. Accounting appealed to me because it is the foundation of all businesses. An accountant's skill set allows him to practice in a variety of specialized fields, including audit, tax, and financial analysis. I chose the audit field because I wanted to understand how businesses function. Accounting was also appealing to me because it provides financial security.

Q. What are your main responsibilities on the job?
A. As an audit senior staff accountant, I am one of many individuals responsible for ensuring that clients' financial statements are

free from material errors. My daily responsibilities include supervising staff, reviewing clients' financial data to ensure that the information accurately reflects their state of business, and utilizing technology to ensure that the clients' systems are secure from tampering and fraud. Auditing also involves meeting client personnel, which at times includes the chief executive officer (CEO) and chief financial officer (CFO), on a regular basis.

Q. **What type of training and education did you pursue to work in this field? Did you complete any internships to prepare for your career?**

A. I graduated from Fordham University with an undergraduate degree in accounting. Subsequent to graduation, I began preparation for the CPA exam in order to become licensed as a certified public accountant. While in college, I interned at Philip Morris International, specifically in their tax department.

Q. **What would you say are the pros and cons of your job?**

A. A pro of audit is that I work in a dynamic environment that keeps the job interesting. An auditor is also given a great deal of responsibility at a young age, which in turn allows one to develop into a strong professional. The significant amount of client interaction also makes the job feel worthwhile.

A con that an auditor faces is deadlines. Every area an auditor works on is usually accompanied by a deadline. In addition, regulatory bodies also set deadlines as to when audit work must be completed.

Q. **What would you say are the most important skills and personal qualities for someone in your field?**

A. Teamwork: Depending on the size of the client, an audit staff usually ranges from three to fifteen individuals. In order to ensure that an audit is completed in a timely manner, it is imperative that each member on the staff be a team player.

Communication: Excellent communication skills are important because auditing also entails facilitating interactions (i.e., phone calls, email, meetings) with various client personnel. An auditor should strive to act in a personable, yet professional, manner when dealing with a client.

Organization: While on an audit engagement, one is usually responsible for performing many tasks. The ability to multi-task and organize are necessary in order to complete one's tasks timely and effectively.

Q. How would someone starting out go about finding work in this field?

A. An individual interested in the audit field should attempt to earn an internship at a Big Four public accounting firm (e.g., Deloitte) during their sophomore year of college. If the public accounting firm of your choice does not provide on-campus recruiting, simply submit a resume directly to the firm's human resources department. Internships usually lead to full-time employment.

Q. What advice would you give to someone who is interested in pursuing this type of career?

A. For someone interested in accounting, I would suggest interning in as many fields related to accounting as possible while in college. And although accounting may sound dull to many, it can actually lead to a variety of excellent job opportunities.

Billing Clerks

OVERVIEW

Billing clerks produce and process bills and collect payments from customers. They enter transactions in business ledgers or spreadsheets, write and send invoices, and verify purchase orders. They are responsible for posting items in accounts payable or receivable, calculating customer charges, and verifying the company's rates for certain products and services. Billing clerks must make sure that all entries are accurate and up-to-date. At the end of the fiscal year, they may work with auditors to clarify billing procedures and answer questions about specific accounts. There are approximately 507,000 billing clerks employed in the United States.

HISTORY

The need to record business transactions has existed ever since people began to engage in business and commerce. As far back as 3000 B.C., Sumerians in Mesopotamia recorded sales and bills for customers on clay tablets. Wealthy traders of early Egyptian and Babylonian civilizations often used slaves to make markings on clay tablets to keep track of purchases and sales.

With the rise of monarchies in Europe, billing clerks were needed to record the business transactions of kings, queens, and rich merchants and to monitor the status of the royal treasury. During the Middle Ages, monks carried out the tasks of billing clerks. As the industrial revolution spread across Europe, increasing commercial transactions, billing clerks became a necessary part of the workforce.

Computer technology has changed the way clerks record transactions today, allowing for billing information and financial transactions to be recorded electronically, eliminating the need for paperwork. But billing clerks continue to occupy a central role in the business world, managing the day-to-day inner workings of company finance.

THE JOB

Billing clerks are responsible for keeping records and up-to-date accounts of all business transactions. They type and send bills for services or products and update files to reflect payments. They also review incoming invoices to ensure that the requested products have been delivered and that the billing statements are accurate and paid on time.

Billing clerks set up shipping and receiving dates. They check customer orders before shipping to make sure they are complete and that all costs, shipping charges, taxes, and credits are included. Billing clerks are also troubleshooters. They contact suppliers or customers when payments are past due or incorrect and help solve the minor problems that invariably occur in the course of business transactions.

Billing clerks enter all transaction information into the firm's account ledger. This ledger lists all the company's transactions such as items bought or sold as well as the credit terms and payment and receiving dates. As payments come in, the billing clerk applies credit to customer accounts and applies any applicable discounts. All correspondence is carefully filed for future reference. Nearly all of this work is done using spreadsheets and computer databases.

The specific duties of billing clerks vary according to the nature of the business in which they work. In an insurance company, the transaction sheet will reflect when and how much customers must pay on their insurance bills. Billing clerks in hospitals compile itemized charges, calculate insurance benefits, and process insurance claims. In accounting, law, and consulting firms, they calculate billable hours and work completed.

Billing clerks are also often responsible for preparing summary statements of financial status, profit-and-loss statements, and payroll lists and deductions. These reports are submitted periodically to company management, who can then gauge the company's financial performance. Clerks may also write company checks, compute federal tax reports, and tabulate personnel profit shares.

Billing clerks may have a specific role within a company. These areas of specialization include the following:

Invoice-control clerks post items in accounts payable or receivable ledgers and verify the accuracy of billing data.

Passenger rate clerks compute fare information for business trips and then provide this information to business personnel.

COD (cash-on-delivery) clerks calculate and record the amount of money collected on COD delivery routes.

Interline clerks compute and pay freight charges for airlines or other transportation agencies that carry freight or passengers as part of a business transaction.

Settlement clerks compute and pay shippers for materials forwarded to a company.

Billing-control clerks compute and pay utility companies for services provided.

Rate reviewers compile data relating to utility costs for management officials.

Services clerks compute and pay tariff charges for boats or ships used to transport materials.

Foreign clerks compute duties, tariffs, and price conversions of exported and imported products.

Billing-machine operators mechanically prepare bills and statements.

Deposit-refund clerks prepare bills for utility customers.

Raters calculate premiums to be paid by customers of insurance companies.

Telegraph-service raters compute costs for sending telegrams.

Billing clerks may work in one specific area or they may be responsible for several areas.

REQUIREMENTS

High School

A high school diploma is usually sufficient for a beginning billing clerk, although business courses in computer operations and bookkeeping are also helpful. In high school, take English, communications, and business writing courses. Computer science and mathematics courses will also prepare you for this career. Some companies test their applicants on math, typing, and computer skills, and others offer on-the-job training.

Postsecondary Training

Community colleges, junior colleges, and vocational schools often offer business education courses that can provide you with additional training.

Other Requirements

If you hope to be a billing clerk, you should have excellent mathematical and organizational skills, be detail oriented, and be able to concentrate on repetitive tasks for long periods of time. In addition, you should be dependable, honest, and trustworthy in dealing with confidential financial matters.

EXPLORING

You can gain experience in this field by taking on clerical or bookkeeping responsibilities with a school club, student government, or other extracurricular activities. If you are interested in the field, you can work in retail operations, either part time or during the summer. Working at the cash register or even pricing products as a stockperson is a good introductory experience. It also may be possible to gain some experience by volunteering to help maintain the bookkeeping records for local groups, such as churches and small businesses.

EMPLOYERS

Employers of billing clerks include hospitals, insurance companies, banks, manufacturers, and utility companies. Of the approximately 507,000 billing clerks employed in the United States, roughly one-third work in the health care field. Wholesale and resale trade industries also employ a large number of billing clerks.

STARTING OUT

Your high school job placement or guidance office can help you find employment opportunities or establish job contacts after you graduate. You may also find specific jobs through classified newspaper advertisements. Most companies provide on-the-job training for entry-level billing clerks to explain to them company procedures and policies and to teach them the basic tasks of the job. During the first month, billing clerks work with experienced personnel.

ADVANCEMENT

Billing clerks usually begin by handling routine tasks such as recording transactions. With experience, they may advance to more complex assignments—which entail computer training in databases and spreadsheets—and assume a greater responsibility for the work as a whole. With additional training and education, billing clerks can be promoted to positions as bookkeepers, accountants, or auditors. Billing clerks with strong leadership and management skills can advance to group manager or supervisor.

There is a high turnover rate in this field, which increases the chance of promotion for employees with ability and initiative.

EARNINGS

Salaries for billing clerks depend on the size and geographic location of the company and the employee's skills. Staring salaries for an employee with little experience may be around $18,000 a year. Full-time billing and posting clerks earned a median hourly wage of $12.55 in 2002, according to the U.S. Department of Labor. For full-time work at 40 hours per week, this hourly wage translates into an annual income of approximately $26,104. Some bill and account collectors may earn a commission based on the number of cases they close in a given time period. Billing clerks with high levels of expertise and management responsibilities may make $38,000 a year or more. Full-time workers also receive paid vacation, health insurance, and other benefits.

WORK ENVIRONMENT

Like most office workers, billing clerks usually work in modern office environments and average 37–40 hours of work per week. Billing clerks spend most of their time behind a desk, and their work can be routine and repetitive. Working long hours in front of a computer can often cause eyestrain, backaches, and headaches, although efforts are being made to reduce physical problems with ergonomically correct equipment. Billing clerks should enjoy systematic and orderly work and have a keen eye for numerical detail. While much of the work is solitary, billing clerks often interact with accountants and management and may work under close supervision.

OUTLOOK

The U.S. Department of Labor predicts that opportunities for billing clerks will grow more slowly than the average through 2012. A number of factors contribute to this slow growth rate. For example, technological advancements—computers, electronic billing, and automated payment methods—will streamline operations and result in the need for fewer workers. The rising popularity of billing via the Internet will also eliminate the number of billing clerks needed in many businesses. Additionally, the responsibilities of billing clerks may be combined with those of other positions. In smaller companies, for example, accounting clerks will make use of billing software, making billing clerks obsolete. Many job openings will result from the need to replace workers who have left for different jobs or other reasons. The health care sector should remain a large employer in this field.

FOR MORE INFORMATION

For additional career information, contact
Office and Professional Employees International Union
265 West 14th Street, 6th Floor
New York, NY 10011
Tel: 800-346-7348
Email: opeiu@opeiu.org
http://www.opeiu.org

Bookkeeping and Accounting Clerks

OVERVIEW

Bookkeeping and accounting clerks record financial transactions for government, business, and other organizations. They compute, classify, record, and verify numerical data in order to develop and maintain accurate financial records. There are approximately 2 million bookkeeping, accounting, and auditing clerks employed in the United States.

HISTORY

The history of bookkeeping developed along with the growth of business and industrial enterprise. The first known records of bookkeeping date back to 2600 B.C., when the Babylonians used pointed sticks to mark accounts on clay slabs. By 3000 B.C., Middle Eastern and Egyptian cultures employed a system of numbers to record merchants' transactions of the grain and farm products that were distributed from storage warehouses. The growth of intricate trade systems brought about the necessity for bookkeeping systems.

Sometime after the start of the 13th century, the decimal numeration system was introduced in Europe, simplifying bookkeeping record systems. The merchants of Venice—one of the busiest trading centers in the world at that time—are credited with the invention of the double-entry bookkeeping method that is widely used today.

As industry in the United States expands and grows more complex, simpler and quicker bookkeeping methods and procedures have evolved. Technological developments include bookkeeping machines, computer hardware and software, and electronic data processing.

THE JOB

Bookkeeping workers keep systematic records and current accounts of financial transactions for businesses, charities, and other organizations. The bookkeeping records of a firm or business are a vital part of its operational procedures because these records reflect the assets and the liabilities, as well as the profits and losses, of the operation.

Bookkeepers record these business transactions daily in spreadsheets on computer databases, and accounting clerks often input the information. The practice of posting accounting records directly onto ledger sheets, in journals, or on other types of written accounting forms is decreasing as computerized recordkeeping becomes more widespread. In small businesses, bookkeepers sort and record all the sales slips, bills, check stubs, inventory lists, and requisition lists. They compile figures for cash receipts, accounts payable and receivable, and profits and losses.

Accounting clerks handle the clerical accounting work; they enter and verify transaction data and compute and record various charges. They may also monitor loans and accounts payable and receivable. More advanced clerks may reconcile billing vouchers, while senior workers review invoices and statements.

Accountants set up bookkeeping systems and use bookkeepers' balance sheets to prepare periodic summary statements of financial transactions. Management relies heavily on these bookkeeping records to interpret the organization's overall performance and uses them to make important business decisions. The records are also necessary to file income tax reports and prepare quarterly reports for stockholders.

Bookkeeping and accounting clerks work in retail and wholesale businesses, manufacturing firms, hospitals, schools, charities, and other types of institutions. Many clerks are classified as financial institution bookkeeping and accounting clerks, insurance firm bookkeeping and accounting clerks, hotel bookkeeping and accounting clerks, and railroad bookkeeping and accounting clerks.

General bookkeepers and *general-ledger bookkeepers* are usually employed in smaller business operations. They may perform all the analysis, maintain the financial records, and complete any other tasks that are involved in keeping a full set of bookkeeping records. These employees may have other general office duties, such as mailing statements, answering telephone calls, and filing materials. *Audit clerks* verify figures and may be responsible for sending them on to an audit clerk supervisor.

In large companies, an accountant may supervise a department of bookkeepers who perform more specialized work. *Billing and rate clerks* and *fixed capital clerks* may post items in accounts payable or receivable ledgers, make out bills and invoices, or verify the company's rates for certain products and services. *Account information clerks* prepare reports, compile payroll lists and deductions, write company checks, and compute federal tax reports or personnel profit shares. Large companies may employ workers to organize, record, and compute many other types of financial information.

In large business organizations, bookkeepers and accountants may be classified by grades, such as bookkeeper I or II. The job classification determines their responsibilities.

REQUIREMENTS

High School

In order to be a bookkeeper, you will need at least a high school diploma. It will be helpful to have a background in business mathematics, business writing, typing, and computer training. Pay particular attention to developing sound English and communication skills along with mathematical abilities.

Postsecondary Training

Although it is not required, having some college experience is becoming increasingly important in this field. Because competition for these jobs can be stiff, candidates with at least an associate's degree in accounting or a related field will have an advantage. Some employers prefer people who have completed a junior college curriculum or those who have attended a post-high-school business-training program. In many instances, employers offer on-the-job training for various types of entry-level positions. In some areas, work-study programs are available in which schools, in cooperation with businesses, offer part-time practical on-the-job training combined with academic study. These programs often help students find immediate employment in similar work after graduation. Local business schools may also offer evening courses.

Other Requirements

Bookkeepers need strong mathematical skills and organizational abilities, and they have to be able to concentrate on detailed work. The work is quite sedentary and often tedious, and you should not mind long hours behind a desk. You should be methodical, accurate, and orderly and enjoy working on detailed tasks. Employers look for honest, discreet, and trustworthy individuals when placing their business in someone else's hands.

Once you are employed as a bookkeeping and accounting clerk, some places of business may require you to have union membership. Larger unions include the Office and Professional Employees International Union; the International Union of Electronics, Electrical, Salaried, Machine, and Furniture Workers; and the American Federation of State, County, and Municipal Employees. Also, depending on the business, clerks may be represented by the same union as other manufacturing employees.

EXPLORING

You can gain experience in bookkeeping by participating in work-study programs or by obtaining part-time or summer work in beginning bookkeeping jobs or related office work. Any retail experience dealing with cash management, pricing, or customer service is also valuable.

You can also volunteer to manage the books for extracurricular student groups. Managing income or cash flow for a club or acting as treasurer for student government are excellent ways to gain experience in maintaining financial records.

Other options are visiting local small businesses to observe their work and talking to representatives of schools that offer business training courses.

EMPLOYERS

Of the approximately 2 million bookkeeping, auditing, and accounting clerks, most work for local governments and for accounting, auditing, and tax-preparation firms. Approximately 25 percent of bookkeeping and accounting clerks work part time, according to the U.S. Department of Labor. Many others are employed by government agencies and organizations that provide educational, health, business, and social services.

STARTING OUT

You may find jobs or establish contacts with businesses that are interested in interviewing graduates through your guidance or placement offices. A work-study program or internship may result in a full-time job offer. Business schools and junior colleges generally provide assistance to their graduates in locating employment.

You may locate job opportunities by applying directly to firms or responding to ads in newspaper classified sections. State employment agencies and private employment bureaus can also assist in the job-search process.

ADVANCEMENT

Bookkeeping workers generally begin their employment by performing routine tasks, such as the simple recording of transactions. Beginners may start as entry-level clerks, cashiers, bookkeeping machine operators, office assistants, or typists. With experience, they may advance to more complex assignments that include computer training in databases and spreadsheets and assume a greater responsibility for the work as a whole.

With experience and education, clerks become department heads or office managers. Further advancement to positions, such as office or division manager, department head, accountant, or auditor, is possible with a college degree and years of experience. There is a high turnover rate in this field, which increases the promotion opportunities for employees with ability and initiative.

EARNINGS

According to the U.S. Department of Labor, bookkeepers and accounting clerks earned a median income of $27,370 a year in 2002. Earnings are also influenced by such factors as the size of the city where they work and the size and type of business for which they are employed. Clerks just starting out earn approximately $18,000. Those with one or two years of college generally earn higher starting wages. Top-paying jobs average about $41,000 or more a year.

Employees usually receive six to eight paid holidays yearly and one week of paid vacation after six to 12 months of service. Paid vacations may increase to four weeks or more, depending on length of service and place of employment. Fringe benefits may include health and life insurance, sick leave, and retirement plans.

WORK ENVIRONMENT

The majority of office workers, including bookkeeping workers, usually work a 40-hour week, although some employees may work a 35–37-hour week. Bookkeeping and accounting clerks usually work in typical office settings. They are more likely to have a cubicle than an office. While the work pace is steady, it can also be routine and repetitive, especially in large companies where the employee is often assigned only one or two specialized job duties.

Attention to numerical details can be physically demanding, and the work can produce eyestrain and nervousness. While bookkeepers usually work with other people and sometimes under close supervision, they can expect to spend most of their day behind a desk; this may seem confining to people who need more variety and stimulation in their work. In addition, the constant attention to detail and the need for accuracy can place considerable responsibility on the worker and cause much stress.

OUTLOOK

Although the growing economy produces a demand for increased accounting services, the automation of office functions will continue to improve overall worker productivity. Fewer people will be needed to do the work, and employment of bookkeeping and accounting clerks is expected to grow more slowly than the average through 2012, according to the U.S. Department of Labor. Excellent computer skills will be vital to securing a job.

Despite lack of growth, there will be numerous replacement job openings, since the turnover rate in this occupation is high. Offices are centralizing their operations, setting up one center to manage all accounting needs in a single location. As more companies trim back their workforces, opportunities for temporary work should continue to grow.

FOR MORE INFORMATION

For information on accredited educational programs, contact
Association to Advance Collegiate Schools of Business
600 Emerson Road, Suite 300
St. Louis, MO 63141
Tel: 314-872-8481
http://www.aacsb.edu

For more information on women in accounting, contact
Educational Foundation for Women in Accounting
PO Box 1925
Southeastern, PA 19399
Tel: 610-407-9229
Email: info@efwa.org
http://www.efwa.org

Business Managers

OVERVIEW

Business managers plan, organize, direct, and coordinate the operations of firms in business and industry. They may oversee an entire company, a geographical territory of a company's operations, or a specific department within a company. Of the 2.7 million managerial jobs in the United States, about 60 percent are found in retail, services, and manufacturing industries.

HISTORY

Everyone has some experience in management. For example, if you schedule your day so that you can get up, get to school on time, go to soccer practice after school, have the time to do your homework, and get to bed at a reasonable hour, you are practicing management skills. Running a household, paying bills, balancing a checkbook, and keeping track of appointments, meetings, and social activities are also examples of managerial activities. Essentially, the term "manage" means to handle, direct, or control.

Management is a necessary part of any enterprise in which a person or group of people are trying to accomplish a specific goal. In fact, civilization could not have grown to its present level of complexity without the planning and organizing involved in effective management. Some of the earliest examples of written documents had to do with the management of business and commerce. As societies and individuals accumulated property and wealth, they needed effective record keeping of taxes, trade agreements, laws, and rights of ownership.

QUICK FACTS

School Subjects
Business
Computer science
Economics

Personal Skills
Helping/teaching
Leadership/management

Work Environment
Primarily indoors
One location with some travel

Minimum Education Level
Bachelor's degree

Salary Range
$45,720 to $68,210 to $145,600+

Certification or Licensing
None available

Outlook
About as fast as the average

DOT
189

GOE
11.05.01

NOC
0611

O*NET-SOC
11-1011.00, 11-1011.02, 11-1021.00, 11-3031.01

The technological advances of the industrial revolution brought about the need for a distinct class of managers. As complex factory systems developed, skilled and trained managers were required to organize and operate them. Workers became specialized in a limited number of tasks, which required managers to coordinate and oversee production.

As businesses began to diversify their production, industries became so complex that their management had to be divided among several different managers, as opposed to one central, authoritarian manager. With the expanded scope of managers and the trend toward decentralized management, the transition to the professional manager took place. In the 1920s, large corporations began to organize with decentralized administration and centralized policy control.

Managers provided a forum for the exchange and evaluation of creative ideas and technical innovations. Eventually these management concepts spread from manufacturing and production to office, personnel, marketing, and financial functions. Today, management is more concerned with results than activities, taking into account individual differences in styles of working.

THE JOB

Management is found in every industry, including food, clothing, banking, education, health care, and business services. All types of businesses have managers to formulate policies and administer the firm's operations. Managers may oversee the operations of an entire company, a geographical territory of a company's operations, or a specific department, such as sales and marketing.

Business managers direct a company's or a department's daily activities within the context of the organization's overall plan. They implement organizational policies and goals. This may involve developing sales or promotional materials, analyzing the department's budgetary requirements, and hiring, training, and supervising staff. Business managers are often responsible for long-range planning for their company or department. This involves setting goals for the organization and developing a workable plan for meeting those goals.

A manager responsible for a single department might work to coordinate his or her department's activities with other departments. A manager responsible for an entire company or organization might work with the managers of various departments or locations to oversee and coordinate the activities of all departments. If the business is privately owned, the owner may be the manager. In a large corporation, however, there will be a management structure above the business manager.

Jeff Bowe is the Midwest General Manager for Disc Graphics, a large printing company headquartered in New York. Bowe oversees all aspects of the company's Indianapolis plant, which employs about 50 people. When asked what he is responsible for, Bowe answers, "Everything that happens in this facility." Specifically, that includes sales, production, customer service, capital expenditure planning, hiring and training employees, firing or downsizing, and personnel management.

The hierarchy of managers includes top executives, such as the *president*, who establishes an organization's goals and policies along with others, such as the chief executive officer, chief financial officer, chief information officer, executive vice president, and the board of directors. Top executives plan business objectives and develop policies to coordinate operations between divisions and departments and establish procedures for attaining objectives. Activity reports and financial statements are reviewed to determine progress and revise operations as needed. The president also directs and formulates funding for new and existing programs within the organization. Public relations plays a big part in the lives of executives as they deal with executives and leaders from other countries or organizations, and with customers, employees, and various special interest groups.

The top-level managers for Bowe's company are located in the company's New York headquarters. Bowe is responsible for reporting certain information about the Indianapolis facility to them. He may also have to work collaboratively with them on certain projects or plans. "I have a conversation with people at headquarters about every two to three days," he says. "I get corporate input on very large projects. I would also work closely with them if we had some type of corporate-wide program we were working on—something where I would be the contact person for this facility."

Although the president or chief executive officer retains ultimate authority and responsibility, Bowe is responsible for overseeing the day-to-day operations of the Indianapolis location. A manager in this position is sometimes called a *chief operating officer* or COO. Other duties of a COO may include serving as chairman of committees, such as management, executive, engineering, or sales.

Some companies have an *executive vice president*, who directs and coordinates the activities of one or more departments, depending on the size of the organization. In very large organizations, the duties of executive vice presidents may be highly specialized. For example, they may oversee the activities of business managers of marketing, sales promotion, purchasing, finance, personnel training, industrial relations, administrative services, data processing, property management, transportation, or legal services. In smaller organizations, an executive vice president might be responsible for a number of these departments. Executive vice presidents also assist the chief executive officer in formulating and administering the organization's policies and developing its long-range goals. Executive vice presidents may serve as members of management committees on special studies.

Companies may also have a *chief financial officer* or *CFO*. In small firms, the CFO is usually responsible for all financial management tasks, such as budgeting, capital expenditure planning, cash flow, and various financial reviews and reports. In larger companies, the CFO may oversee financial management departments, to help other managers develop financial and economic policy and oversee the implementation of these policies.

Chief information officers, or *CIOs,* are responsible for all aspects of their company's information technology. They use their knowledge of technology and business to determine how information technology can best be used to meet company goals. This may include researching, purchasing, and overseeing the setup and use of technology systems, such as Intranet, Internet, and computer networks. These managers sometimes take a role in implementing a company's website.

In companies that have several different locations, managers may be assigned to oversee specific geographic areas. For example, a large retailer with facilities all across the nation is likely to have a number of managers in charge of various territories. There might be a Midwest manager, a Southwest manager, a Southeast manager, a Northeast manager, and a Northwest manager. These managers are often called *regional* or *area managers.* Some companies break their management territories up into even smaller sections, such as a single state or a part of a state. Managers overseeing these smaller segments are often called *district managers* and typically report directly to an area or regional manager.

REQUIREMENTS

High School

The educational background of business managers varies as widely as the nature of their diverse responsibilities. Many have a bachelor's degree in liberal arts or business administration. If you are interested in a business managerial career, you should start preparing in high school by taking college preparatory classes. According to Jeff Bowe, your best bet academically is to get a well-rounded education. Because communication is important, take as many English classes as possible. Speech classes are another way to improve your communication skills. Courses in mathematics, business, and computer science are also excellent choices to help you prepare for this career. Finally, Bowe recommends taking a foreign language. "Today, speaking a foreign language is more and more important," he says. "Which language is not so important. Any of the global languages are something you could very well use, depending upon where you end up."

Postsecondary Training

Business managers often have a college degree in a subject that pertains to the department they direct or the organization they administer; for example, accounting or economics for a business manager of finance, computer science for a business manager of data processing, engineering or science for a director of research and development. As computer usage grows, many managers are expected to have experience with the information technology that applies to their field.

Graduate and professional degrees are common. Bowe, along with many managers in administrative, marketing, financial, and manufacturing activities, has a master's degree in business administration. Managers in highly technical manufacturing and research activities often have a master's degree or doctorate in a technical or scientific discipline. A law degree is mandatory for business managers of corporate legal departments, and hospital managers generally have a master's degree in health services administration or business administration. In some industries, such as retail trade or the food and beverage industry, competent individuals without a college degree but who have extensive experience in their field may become business managers.

Other Requirements

There are a number of personal characteristics that help one be a successful business manager, depending upon the specific responsibilities of the position. A manager who oversees other employees should have good communication and interpersonal skills. The ability to delegate work is another important personality trait of a good manager. The ability to think on your feet is often key in business management, according to Bowe. "You have to be able to think extremely quickly and not in a reactionary manner," he says. Bowe also says that a certain degree of organization is important, since managers are often managing several different things simultaneously. Other traits considered important for

Magazines for Managers

Most successful business managers try to keep up-to-date with current happenings in the business world by reading daily newspapers and business-related magazines. To get a taste of what managers read, browse through some of the following periodicals:

Business Week (http://www.businessweek.com)

CIO (http://www.cio.com)

Chief Executive (http://www.chiefexecutive.net)

The Economist (http://www.economist.com)

Fast Company (http://www.fastcompany.com)

Fortune (http://www.fortune.com)

Forbes (http://www.forbes.com)

Inc. (http://www.inc.com)

Industry Week (http://www.iwgc.com)

Newsweek (http://www.newsweek.com)

U.S. News & World Report (http://www.usnews.com)

Wall Street Journal (http://www.wsj.com)

top executives are intelligence, decisiveness, intuition, creativity, honesty, loyalty, a sense of responsibility, and planning abilities. Finally, the successful manager should be flexible and interested in staying abreast of new developments in his or her industry. "In general, you need to be open to change because your customers change, your market changes, your technology changes," he says. "If you won't try something new, you really have no business being in management."

EXPLORING

To get experience as a manager, start with your own interests. Whether you're involved in drama, sports, school publications, or a part-time job, there are managerial duties associated with any organized activity. These can involve planning, scheduling, managing other workers or volunteers, fund-raising, or budgeting. Local businesses also have job opportunities through which you can get firsthand knowledge and experience of management structure. If you can't get an actual job, at least try to schedule a meeting with a business manager to talk with him or her about the career. Some schools or community organizations arrange job-shadowing, where you can spend part of a day following a selected employee to see what his or her job is like. Joining Junior Achievement is another excellent way to get involved with local businesses and learn about how they work. Finally, take every opportunity to work with computers, since computer skills are vital to today's business world.

EMPLOYERS

There are approximately 2.7 million general managers and executives employed in the United States. These jobs are found in every industry, but almost 60 percent of business managers work in service-related industries.

Virtually every business in the United States has some form of managerial positions. Obviously, the larger the company is, the more managerial positions it is likely to have. Another factor is the geographical territory covered by the business. It is safe to say that companies doing business in larger geographical territories are likely to have more managerial positions than those with smaller territories.

STARTING OUT

Generally you will need a college degree for this career, although many retail stores, grocery stores, and restaurants hire promising applicants who have only a high school diploma. Job seekers usually apply directly to the manager of such places. Your college placement office is often the best place to start looking for these positions. A number of listings can also be found in newspaper help wanted ads.

Many organizations have management-trainee programs that college graduates can enter. Such programs are advertised at college career fairs or through college job placement services. However, management-trainee positions in business and government are often filled by employees who are already working for the organization and who demonstrate management potential. Jeff Bowe suggests researching the industry you are interested in to find out what might be the best point of entry for that field. "I came into the printing company through customer service, which is a good point of entry because it's one of the easiest things to learn," he says. "Although it requires more technical know-how now than it did then, customer service is still not a bad entry point for this industry."

ADVANCEMENT

Most business management and top executive positions are filled by experienced lower level managers and executives who display valuable managerial traits, such as leadership, self-confidence, creativity, motivation, decisiveness, and flexibility. In small firms advancement to a higher management position may come slowly, while promotions may occur more quickly in larger firms.

Advancement may be accelerated by participating in different kinds of educational programs available for managers. These are often paid for by the organization. Company training programs broaden knowledge of company policy and operations. Training programs sponsored by industry and trade associations and continuing education courses in colleges and universities can familiarize managers with the latest developments in management techniques. In recent years, large numbers of middle managers were laid off as companies streamlined operations. Competition for jobs is keen, and business managers committed to improving their knowledge of the field and of related disciplines—especially computer information systems—will have the best opportunities for advancement.

Business managers may advance to executive or administrative vice president. Vice presidents may advance to peak corporate positions—president or chief executive officer. Presidents and chief executive officers, upon retirement, may become members of the board of directors of one or more firms. Sometimes business managers establish their own firms.

EARNINGS

Salary levels for business managers vary substantially, depending upon the level of responsibility, length of service, and type, size, and location of the organization. Top-level managers in large businesses are among today's highest paid workers and can earn much more than their counterparts in small firms. Also, salaries in large metropolitan areas, such as New York City, are higher than those in smaller cities.

According to the U.S. Department of Labor, general managers had a median yearly income of $68,210 in 2002. The middle 50 percent of managers made between $45,720 and $104,970. As you can see, earnings vary considerably.

Chief executives earned a median of $126,260 annually in 2002. And again, salaries varied by industry. Managers of large businesses such as public relations firms made $145,600, while managers at colleges and universities made $103,120. A survey by Abbott, Langer, & Associates found that chief executives working for nonprofits had a median yearly salary of $81,000 in 2003. Some executives, however, earn hundreds of thousands of dollars more than this annually.

Benefit and compensation packages for business managers are usually excellent, and may even include such things as bonuses, stock awards, company-paid insurance premiums, use of company cars, paid country club memberships, expense accounts, and generous retirement benefits.

WORK ENVIRONMENT

Business managers are provided with comfortable offices near the departments they direct. Top executives may have spacious, lavish offices and may enjoy such privileges as executive dining rooms, company cars, country club memberships, and liberal expense accounts.

Managers often travel between national, regional, and local offices. Top executives may travel to meet with executives in other corporations, both within the United States and abroad. Meetings and conferences sponsored by industries and associations occur regularly and provide invaluable opportunities to meet with peers and keep up with the latest developments. In large corporations, job transfers between the parent company and its local offices or subsidiaries are common.

Business managers often work long hours under intense pressure to meet, for example, production and marketing goals. Jeff Bowe's average workweek consists of 55–60 hours at the office. This is not uncommon—in fact, some executives spend up to 80 hours working each week. These long hours limit time available for family and leisure activities.

OUTLOOK

Overall, employment of business managers and executives is expected to grow about as fast as the average through 2012, according to the U.S. Bureau of Labor Statistics. Many job openings will be the result of managers being promoted to better positions, retiring, or leaving their positions to start their own businesses. Even so, the compensation and prestige of these positions make them highly sought-after, and competition to fill openings will be intense.

Projected employment growth varies by industry. For example, employment in science and technology should increase faster than the average, while employment in some manufacturing industries is expected to decline.

The outlook for business managers is closely tied to the overall economy. When the economy is good, businesses expand both in terms of their output and the number of people they employ, which creates a need for more managers. In economic downturns, businesses often lay off employees and cut back on production, which lessens the need for managers.

FOR MORE INFORMATION

For news about management trends, resources on career information and finding a job, and an online job bank, contact
American Management Association
1601 Broadway
New York, NY 10019
Tel: 800-262-9699
http://www.amanet.org

For brochures on careers in management for women, contact
Association for Women in Management
927 15th Street, NW, Suite 1000
Washington, DC 20005
Tel: 202-659-6364
Email: awm@benefits.net
http://www.womens.org

For information about programs for students in kindergarten through high school and information on local chapters, contact
Junior Achievement
One Education Way
Colorado Springs, CO 80906
Tel: 719-540-8000
Email: newmedia@ja.org
http://www.ja.org

For a brochure on management as a career, contact
National Management Association
2210 Arbor Boulevard
Dayton, OH 45439
Tel: 937-294-0421
http://nma1.org

Cultural Advisers

QUICK FACTS

School Subjects
Business
Foreign language
Speech

Personal Skills
Communication/ideas
Helping/teaching

Work Environment
Primarily indoors
Primarily multiple
locations

Minimum Education Level
Bachelor's degree

Salary Range
$65 to $100 to $265 per
hour

Certification or Licensing
None available

Outlook
Faster than the average

DOT
N/A

GOE
N/A

NOC
N/A

O*NET-SOC
N/A

OVERVIEW

Cultural advisers, also known as *bilingual consultants,* work with businesses and organizations to help them communicate effectively with others who are from different cultural and linguistic backgrounds. Cultural advisers usually have a specialty such as business management, banking, education, or computer technology. They help bridge both language and cultural barriers in our increasingly global business world.

HISTORY

Communication has always been a challenge when cultures come into contact with each other. In the early days of the United States, settlers and explorers relied on interpreters to assist them. One of those famous interpreters, Sacajawea, a member of the Shoshone Indian tribe, was a precursor of the cultural advisers of today. As she helped guide Meriwether Lewis and William Clark across the West to the Pacific Ocean, she acted as interpreter when they encountered Native American tribes. She also helped the explorers adapt to different cultures and customs.

Today's cultural advisers work with companies or organizations that need to communicate effectively and do business with other cultures. Cultural advisers are becoming even more valuable because it is now relatively quick and easy to travel throughout the world. Each year, more trade barriers are broken down by legislation, such as the North American Free Trade Agreement, implemented in 1994.

Words to Learn

bilingual: fluent in two languages

consultant: professional who offers advice, knowledge, and training

culture: set of precedents and traditions that signify a people's heritage

custom: usual course of action, often particular to a certain country or culture

international: referring to two or more nations

interpreter: person who translates words from one language to another

language: using words to communicate

NAFTA: The North American Free Trade Agreement, passed in 1994 that increased free trade opportunities among North American countries

THE JOB

Cultural advisers work to bridge gaps in communication and culture. They usually have a second specialty that is complimented by their bilingual skills. For example, a banking and finance expert who has traveled extensively in Japan and is familiar with Japanese language and customs would have the marketable skills to become a cultural adviser for American companies interested in doing business in Japan.

Cultural advisers work in a wide variety of settings. They may hold full-time staff positions with organizations or they may work as independent consultants providing services to a number of clients. Cultural advisers work in education. They provide translation services and help foreign or immigrant students adjust to a new culture. They also educate teachers and administrators to make them aware of cultural differences, so that programs and classes can be adapted to include everyone. Colleges and universities that have large international student populations often have cultural advisers on staff.

In industry, cultural advisers train workers in safety procedures and worker rights. The health care industry benefits from the use of advisers to communicate with non-English-speaking patients. Cultural advisers also hold training sessions for health care professionals to teach them how to better understand and instruct their patients.

Large business enterprises that have overseas interests hire cultural advisers to research new markets and help with negotiations. Some advisers work primarily in employment, finding foreign experts to work for American businesses or finding overseas jobs for American

A cultural adviser translates a memo for two clients. *(Getty Images)*

workers. In addition to advising American business leaders, cultural advisers sometimes work with foreign entities who want to do business in the United States. They provide English language instruction and training in American business practices.

Cultural advisers also work in the legal system, the media, advertising, the travel industry, social services, and government agencies. Whatever the setting, cultural advisers help their clients—foreign and domestic—understand and respect other cultures and communicate effectively with each other.

REQUIREMENTS

High School

Classes in business, speech, and foreign language will give you an excellent head start to becoming a cultural adviser. In addition, take other classes in your high school's college-prep curriculum. These courses should include history, mathematics, sciences, and English. Accounting classes and computer science classes will also help prepare you for working in business.

Postsecondary Training

If you are planning a career as a cultural adviser, fluency in two or more languages is a requirement; thus, you should probably major or minor in a foreign language in college. Courses in business, world history, world geography, and sociology would be useful as well. You will need at least a bachelor's degree to find work as a cultural adviser, and you may want to consider pursuing a master's degree to have more job opportunities. Many universities offer programs in cultural studies, and there are master's programs that offer a concentration in international business.

Take advantage of every opportunity to learn about the people and area you want to work with. Studying abroad for a semester or year is also recommended.

Other Requirements

Cultural sensitivity is the number-one requirement for an adviser. Knowing the history, culture, and social conventions of a people as well as the language is a very important part of the job. Also, expertise in another area, such as business, education, law, or computers, is necessary to be a cultural adviser.

EXPLORING

A good way to explore this field is to join one of your high school's foreign language clubs. In addition to using the foreign language, these clubs often have activities related to the culture where the language is spoken. You may also find it helpful to join your school's business club, which will give you an opportunity to learn about business tactics and finances, as well as give you an idea of how to run your own business.

Learn as much as you can about people and life in other parts of the world. You can do this by joining groups such as American Field Service International (AFS) and getting to know a student from another country who is attending your school. There are also study and living abroad programs you can apply to even while in high school. Rotary International and AFS offer such opportunities; see the end of the article for contact information.

EMPLOYERS

Cultural advisers are employed on a contract or project basis by businesses, associations, and educational institutions. Large global companies are the most significant source of employment for cultural advisers as they seek to serve the global population. Small to medium-sized companies that do business in a particular region also employ cultural advisers.

Companies in large cities offer the most opportunities for cultural advisers, especially those cities that border other countries.

Miguel Orta is a cultural adviser in North Miami Beach, Florida. He works with Latin American companies and American companies doing business in Central America and South America. He also has a background in law and business management. Orta is fluent in English, Spanish, and Portuguese. He uses his location in Florida to help businesses in the United States interact with a growing Hispanic population. His Florida location also allows him to be only a short plane flight from his Latin American clients.

STARTING OUT

Most cultural advisers do not begin this career right after college. Some real-life experience is necessary to be qualified to fill the cultural adviser's role. "Education is very important," says Miguel Orta. "But first you need some work in the trenches." Once that experience is obtained, you will be ready to try advising.

After graduating with a law degree, Orta spent several years as a private attorney representing many Latin American clients. He practiced corporate, international, and labor law. When the opportunity came to serve one of his Venezuelan clients as a cultural adviser, Orta enjoyed the work and decided to become an adviser to others in need of those services.

ADVANCEMENT

Working with larger companies on more extensive projects is one way for a cultural adviser to advance. If an adviser decides to trade in the flexibility and freedom of the job, opportunities to become a salaried employee would most likely be available.

EARNINGS

Cultural advisers are well compensated for the time they spend on projects. Rates can range from approximately $65 to as high as $265 per hour. The median rate is close to $100 per hour. Advisers may incur business expenses, but their clients generally pay many of the expenses associated with the work, such as travel, meals, and lodging.

WORK ENVIRONMENT

The work environment of cultural advisers largely depends on their specialties. A smaller company may offer a more informal setting than a multinational corporation. A cultural adviser who is employed by a large, international bank may travel much more than an adviser who works for an educational institution or association.

While cultural advisers generally work independently on projects, they must also communicate with a large number of people to complete their tasks. In the middle of a project, a cultural adviser may work 50–60 hours per week and travel may be necessary. Between projects, cultural advisers manage their businesses and solicit new clients.

OUTLOOK

The field of cultural advising is predicted to grow faster than average in the next decade. Demand will grow as trade barriers are continually loosened and U.S. companies conduct more business on a global scale. Latin America and Asia are two promising areas for American businesses.

Cultural advisers will also be needed to address the interests of the increasingly diverse population of the United States. However, competition is keen, and those with graduate degrees and specific expertise will be the most successful.

FOR MORE INFORMATION

Management consulting firms employ a large number of cultural advisers. For more information on the consulting business, contact

Association of Career Management Consulting Firms International
204 E Street, NE
Washington, DC 20002
Tel: 202-547-6344
Email: aocfi@aocfi.org
http://www.aocfi.org

For information about cultural exchanges, contact the following

American Field Service International
71 West 23rd Street, 17th Floor
New York, NY 10010
Tel: 212-807-8686
Email: info@afs.org
http://www.afs.org

Rotary International
One Rotary Center
1560 Sherman Avenue
Evanston, IL 60201
Tel: 847-866-3000
http://www.rotary.org

For information on etiquette and cross-cultural training, contact

Multi-Language Consultants, Inc.
Tel: 212-726-2164
Email: contact@mlc.com
http://www.mlc.com

Protocol Advisors, Inc.
241 Beacon Street
Boston, MA 02116
Tel: 617-267-6950
http://www.protocoladvisors.com

Customer Service Representatives

OVERVIEW

Customer service representatives, sometimes called customer care representatives, work with customers of one or many companies, assisting with customer problems and answering questions. Customer service representatives work in many different industries to provide "front-line" customer service in a variety of businesses. Most customer service representatives work in an office setting though some may work in the "field" to better meet customer needs. There are approximately 1.9 million customer service representatives employed in the United States.

HISTORY

Customer service has been a part of business for many years; however, the formal title of customer service representative is relatively new. More than a decade ago, the International Customer Service Association established Customer Service Week to recognize and promote customer service.

In 1992, President George Bush made the week a national event. "If the United States is to remain a leader in the changing global economy, highest quality customer service must be a personal goal of every employee in business and industry," said the president in his proclamation.

As the world moves toward a more global and competitive economic market, customer service, along with quality control, has taken a front seat in the business world. Serving customers and serving them well is more important now than ever before.

Customer service is about communication, so the progress in customer service can be tied closely to the progress in the communication industry. When Alexander Graham Bell invented the telephone in 1876, he probably did not envision the customer service lines, automated response messages, and toll-free phone numbers that now help customer service representatives do their jobs.

The increased use of the Internet has helped companies serve and communicate with their customers in another way. From the simple email complaint form to online help files, companies are using the Internet to provide better customer service. Some companies even have online chat capabilities to communicate with their customers instantaneously on the Web.

THE JOB

Julie Cox is a customer service representative for Affina, a call center that handles customer service for a variety of companies. Cox works with each of Affina's clients and the call center operators to ensure that each call-in receives top customer service.

Customer service representatives often handle complaints and problems, and Cox finds that to be the case at the call center as well. While the operators who report to her provide customer service to those on the phone, Cox must oversee that customer service while also keeping in mind the customer service for her client, whatever business they may be in.

"I make sure that the clients get regular reports of the customer service calls and check to see if there are any recurring problems," says Cox.

One of the ways Cox observes if customer service is not being handled effectively is by monitoring the actual time spent on each phone call. If an operator spends a lot of time on a call, there is most likely a problem.

"Our customers are billed per minute," says Cox. "So we want to make sure their customer service is being handled well and efficiently."

Affina's call center in Columbus, Indiana, handles dozens of toll-free lines. While some calls are likely to be focused on complaints or questions, some are easier to handle. Cox and her staff handle calls from people simply wanting to order literature, brochures, or to find their nearest dealer location.

Customer service representatives work in a variety of fields and business, but one thing is common—the customer. All businesses depend on their customers to keep them in business, so customer service, whether handled internally or outsourced to a call center like Affina, is extremely important.

Maintaining a positive and helpful attitude is a key element in customer service. *(Getty Images)*

Some customer service representatives, like Cox, do most of their work on the telephone. Others may represent companies in the field, where the customer is actually using the product or service. Still other customer service representatives may specialize in Internet service, assisting customers over the World Wide Web via email or online chats.

Affina's call center is available to their clients 24 hours a day, seven days a week, so Cox and her staff must keep around-the-clock shifts. Not all customer service representatives work a varied schedule; many work a traditional daytime shift. However, customers have problems, complaints, and questions 24 hours a day, so many companies do staff their customer service positions for a longer number of hours, especially to accommodate customers during evenings and weekends.

REQUIREMENTS

High School

A high school diploma is required for most customer service representative positions. High school courses that emphasize communication, such as English and speech, will help you learn to communicate clearly. Any courses that require collaboration with others will also help to teach diplomacy and tact—two important aspects of customer service. Business courses will help you get a good overview of the business world, one that is dependent on customers and customer service. Computer skills are also very important.

Postsecondary Training

While a college degree is not necessary to become a customer service representative, certain areas of postsecondary training are helpful. Courses in business and organizational leadership will help to give you a better feel for the business world. Just as in high school, communications classes are helpful in learning to talk effectively with and meet the needs of other people.

These courses can be taken during a college curriculum or may be offered at a variety of customer service workshops or classes. Julie Cox is working as a customer service representative while she earns her business degree from a local college. Along with her college work, she has taken advantage of seminars and workshops to improve her customer service skills.

Bachelor's degrees in business and communications are increasingly required for managerial positions.

Certification or Licensing

Although it is not a requirement, customer service representatives can become certified. The International Customer Service Association offers a manager-level certification program. Upon completion of the program, managers receive the certified customer service professional designation.

Other Requirements

"The best and the worst parts of being a customer service representative are the people," Julie Cox says. Customer service representa-

Working for Perfection

Some may think that 99.9 percent is good enough for the customer, but according to the International Customer Service Association (ICSA), if that were true, then

- 2 million documents would be lost by the IRS this year

- 1,314 phone calls would be misplaced by telecommunication companies each minute

- 12 babies would be given to the wrong parents each day

- 315 entries in Webster's *Third New International Dictionary of the English Language* would be misspelled

Customer service representatives aim for 100 percent accuracy because 99.9 percent is not good enough to provide customer satisfaction.

tives should have the ability to maintain a pleasant attitude at all times, even while serving angry or demanding customers.

A successful customer service representative will most likely have an outgoing personality and enjoy working with people and assisting them with their questions and problems.

Because many customer service representatives work in offices and on the telephone, people with physical disabilities may find this career to be both accessible and enjoyable.

EXPLORING

Julie Cox first discovered her love for customer service while working in retail at a local department store. Explore your ability for customer service by getting a job that deals with the public on a day-to-day basis. Talk with people who work with customers and customer service every day; find out what they like and dislike about their jobs.

There are other ways that you can prepare for a career in this field while you are still in school. Join your school's business club to get a feel for what goes on in the business world today. Doing volunteer work for a local charity or homeless shelter can help you decide if serving others is something that you'd enjoy doing as a career.

Evaluate the customer service at the businesses you visit. What makes that salesperson at The Gap better than the operator you talked with last week? Volunteer to answer phones at an agency in your town or city. Most receptionists in small companies and agencies are called on to provide customer service to callers. Try a nonprofit organization. They will welcome the help, and you will get a firsthand look at customer service.

EMPLOYERS

Customer service representatives are hired at all types of companies in a variety of areas. Because all businesses rely on customers, customer service is generally a high priority for those businesses. Some companies, like call centers, may employ a large number of customer service representatives to serve a multitude of clients, while small businesses may simply have one or two people who are responsible for customer service.

Geography makes little difference when it comes to customer service. Smaller businesses may not be able to hire a person to handle customer service exclusively, but most businesses will have people designated to meet customer's needs. In the United States, approximately 1.9 million workers are employed as customer service representatives.

STARTING OUT

You can become a customer service representative as an entry-level applicant, although some customer service representatives have first served in other areas of a company. This company experience may provide them with more knowledge and experience to answer customer questions. A college degree is not required, but any postsecondary training will increase your ability to find a job in customer service.

Ads for customer service job openings are readily available in newspapers and on Internet job search sites. With some experience and a positive attitude, it is possible to move into the position of customer service representative from another job within the company. Julie Cox started out at Affina as an operator and quickly moved into a customer service capacity.

ADVANCEMENT

Customer service experience is valuable in any business career path. Julie Cox hopes to combine her customer service experience with a business degree and move to the human resources area of her company.

It is also possible to advance to management or marketing jobs after working as a customer service representative. Businesses and their customers are inseparable, so most business professionals are experts at customer relations.

EARNINGS

Earnings vary based on location, level of experience, and size and type of employer. The U.S. Department of Labor reports the median annual income for all customer service representatives as $26,240 in 2002. Salaries ranged from $17,230 to more than $42,990. Customer service representatives for wired telecommunications carriers earned the highest median annual salaries: $38,980 a year.

Other benefits vary widely according to the size and type of company in which representatives are employed. Benefits may include medical, dental, vision, and life insurance, 401(k) plans, or bonus incentives. Full-time customer service representatives can expect to receive vacation and sick pay, while part-time workers may not be offered these benefits.

WORK ENVIRONMENT

Customer service representatives work primarily indoors, although some may work in the field where the customers are using the product or service. They usually work in a supervised setting and report to a manager. They may spend many hours on the telephone, answering mail, or handling Internet communication. Many of the work hours involve little physical activity.

While most customer service representatives generally work a 40-hour workweek, others work a variety of shifts. Many businesses want customer service hours to coincide with the times that their customers are available to call or contact the business. For many companies, these times are in the evenings and on the weekends, so some customer service representatives work varied shifts and odd hours.

OUTLOOK

The U.S. Department of Labor predicts that employment for customer service representatives will grow faster than the average through 2012. This is a large field of workers and many replacement workers are needed each year as customer service reps leave this job for other positions, retire, or leave for other reasons. In addition, the Internet and ecommerce should increase the need for customer service representatives who will be needed to help customers navigate websites, answer questions over the phone, and respond to emails.

For customer service representatives with specific knowledge of a product or business, the outlook is very good, as quick, efficient customer service is valuable in any business. Given the increasingly complex nature of business, customer service representatives may be given additional duties, such as cross-selling products and opening new accounts. Additional training and education will also make finding a job as a customer service representative an easier task. Job candidates who speak more than one language will be in particularly high demand.

FOR MORE INFORMATION

For information on customer service and other support positions, contact
Association of Support Professionals
122 Barnard Avenue
Watertown, MA 02472
Tel: 617-924-3944
http://www.asponline.com

For information on jobs, training, workshops, and salaries, contact
Customer Care Institute
17 Dean Overlook, NW
Atlanta, GA 30318
Tel: 404-352-9291
Email: info@customercare.com
http://www.customercare.com

For information about the customer service industry, contact
Help Desk Institute
6385 Corporate Drive, Suite 301
Colorado Springs, CO 80919
Tel: 800-248-5667
Email: support@thinkhdi.com
http://www.helpdeskinst.com

For information on international customer service careers, contact
International Customer Service Association
401 North Michigan Avenue
Chicago, IL 60611
Tel: 800-360-4272
Email: icsa@sba.com
http://www.icsa.com

Data Entry Clerks

QUICK FACTS

School Subjects
Business
Computer science
English

Personal Skills
Following instructions
Mechanical/manipulative

Work Environment
Primarily indoors
Primarily one location

Minimum Education Level
High school diploma

Salary Range
$15,910 to $22,390 to
$26,840+

Certification or Licensing
None available

Outlook
Decline

DOT
203

GOE
07.06.01

NOC
1422

O*NET-SOC
43-9021.00

OVERVIEW

Data entry clerks transfer information from paper documents to a computer system. They use either a typewriter-like (alphanumeric) keyboard or a 10-key (numerals only) pad to enter data into the system. In this way, the data is converted into a form the computer can easily read and process. There are about 633,000 data entry and information processing workers in the United States.

HISTORY

Following World War II, the electronic technology that had been used during the war was transferred to government and business sectors for use in peacetime operations. This technology included one of the earliest computers. The first all-purpose electronic digital computer was named ENIAC. Developed at the University of Pennsylvania in 1946, it relied on thousands of vacuum tubes like the ones used in the first television sets and radios. In 1951, UNIVAC became the first computer that could handle large amounts of both numeric and alphabetic data easily.

In the 1960s, the invention of the transistor made it possible to build smaller, more powerful computers. Computers designed specifically for home use were introduced in the 1970s. As the computer field continued to produce faster, more efficient, and more powerful computers, the capacity of the machines to read, store, process, and organize information increased dramatically. By the late 1970s computers were indispensable to private companies, schools, hospitals, and government agencies, all of which rely on vast amounts of information.

Today, all types of organizations use computers to process and organize many different kinds of data and information. Hospitals maintain computerized patient records and schools automate student transcripts. This boom in computerized information processing has created the need for qualified data entry clerks.

THE JOB

Data entry clerks are responsible for entering data into computer systems so that the information can be processed at various times to produce important business documents such as sales reports, billing invoices, mailing lists, and many others. Specific job responsibilities vary according to the type of computer system being used and the nature of the employer. For example, a data entry clerk may enter financial information for use at a bank, merchandising information for use at a store, or scientific information for use at a research laboratory.

From a source document such as a financial statement, data entry clerks type in information in either alphabetic, numeric, or symbolic code. The information is entered using a keyboard, either the regular typewriter-like computer keyboard or a more customized keypad developed for a certain industry or business. The entry machine converts the coded information into either electronic impulses or a series of holes in a tape that the computer can read and process electronically. Newer, more sophisticated computers have eliminated the need for magnetic tapes, however, and rely exclusively on computer files. Some data entry work does not involve inputting actual information but rather entering special instructions that tell the computer what functions to perform and when.

In small companies, data entry clerks may combine data entry responsibilities with general office work. Because of staff limitations, clerks may have to know and be able to operate several types of computer systems. Larger companies tend to assign data entry clerks to one type of entry machinery. For example, data entry clerks in a check or credit processing center might be assigned solely to changing client addresses in the company database or entering payment amounts from individual checks.

Some data entry clerks are responsible for setting up their entry machines according to the type of input data. Clerks who handle vast amounts of financial data, for example, set their machines to automatically record a series of numbers as dollar amounts or transaction dates without having to input dollar signs or hyphens. The special setups reduce the number of strokes data entry clerks have to perform in order to finish one transaction, thereby increasing productivity. Some data entry clerks may be responsible for loading the appropriate tape or other material into their machines and selecting the correct coding system (that is, the alphabetic, numeric, or symbolic representations).

Accuracy is an essential element of all data entry work. If a customer pays $100 toward a credit card bill but the clerk records a payment of only $10, the company will experience problems down the line. Therefore, most companies have an extensive series of accuracy checks and error tests designed to detect as many errors as possible. Some tests are computerized, checking entries against information that is expected for the given type of work or is scanned in directly from source documents. Data entry clerks must always verify their own work as well. They consistently check their computer screens for obvious errors and systematically refer back to the source documents to ensure that they entered the information correctly. Sometimes *verifier operators* are employed specifically to perform accuracy tests of previously processed information. Such tests may be random or complete, depending on the nature and scope of the work. When verifier operators find mistakes, they correct them and later prepare accuracy reports for each data entry clerk.

Data typists and *keypunch operators* formerly prepared data for computer input by punching data into special coding cards or paper tapes. The cards were punched on machines that resembled typewriters. When tapes were used, the work was done on machines such as bookkeeping or adding machines that had special attachments to perforate paper tape. The use of cards and tape is decreasing substantially as electronic databases become more flexible, fast, and efficient. Consequently, most data typists and keypunch operators working today are basically doing data entry work at terminals similar to those of other data entry clerks.

Data-coder operators examine the information in the source material to determine what codes and symbols should be used to enter it into the computer. They may write the operating instructions for the data entry staff and assist the system programmer in testing and revising computer programs designed to process data entry work. Data-coder operators might also assist programmers in preparing detailed flowcharts of how the information is being stored and used in the computer system and in designing coded computer instructions to fulfill business needs.

Terminal operators also use coding systems to input information from the source document into a series of alphabetic or numeric signals that can be read by the computer. After checking their work for accuracy, they send the data to the computer system via telephone lines or other remote-transmission methods if they do not input directly into the computer network.

REQUIREMENTS

High School

In high school, you should take English, typing, computer science, and other business courses that focus on the operation of office machinery. A high school diploma is usually required for data entry work. In a growing number of cases, some college training is desirable. Most data entry clerks receive on-the-job training pertaining specifically to the computer system and input procedures used by the employer. Before you begin your first job as a data entry clerk, you should be able to quickly scan documents and type the information you read.

Postsecondary Training

Many aspiring data entry clerks now complete data processing courses that instruct students on proper inputting methods and other skills needed for the job. Technical schools, community colleges, business schools, and some adult education programs offer courses related to data processing. These courses are generally between six months and two years in duration. Secretarial or business schools may also offer data entry courses.

Other Requirements

Most companies test prospective employees to evaluate their typing skills in terms of both speed and accuracy. Competency in general mathematics and spelling is frequently reviewed as well. You must be accurate and highly productive, capable of inputting several hundred pieces of information per hour, and you must be comfortable with the high degree of routine and repetition involved in your daily tasks. As computers continue to change, you must always be ready to learn new methods and techniques of input.

EXPLORING

If you are interested in pursuing a career in data entry, you should discuss the field with individuals who are already employed as clerks. A visit to an office that uses data processing systems may provide a good opportunity to learn more about the rewards and drawbacks of this position. Secretarial work or similar office work may also help you understand what data entry work involves. At home or school, you can practice typing by using a computer or typewriter or by entering data for various club or group activities.

EMPLOYERS

Approximately 633,000 data entry clerks are employed in the United States. Of these workers, about 392,000 are data entry keyers and 241,000 are word processors and typists. Major employers of data entry clerks include insurance companies, utilities, banks, credit or check clearinghouses, mail-order catalogs, temporary employment agencies, and manufacturing firms. The federal government operates its own training program for data entry clerks. Applications for such positions may be made through the Office of Personnel Management.

STARTING OUT

Many people entering the field have already completed an educational program at a technical school or other institution that provides data processing training. Job placement counselors at these schools are often very helpful in locating employment opportunities for qualified applicants.

Local and state employment offices as well as classified advertisements list job openings. You may also make direct contact with area employers who maintain large data processing departments, as there tends to be a rather high turnover in this field.

ADVANCEMENT

Data entry positions are considered entry-level jobs, and as such, data entry itself does not offer tremendous potential for growth. Data entry clerks may be promoted to working on more complicated machines or systems, but the work is basically the same. Better opportunities arise when data entry clerks use their computer experience and training to springboard to higher-level positions. For example, skilled data entry clerks may be promoted to supervisory positions in which they are responsible for overseeing the data processing department or a team of clerks. Duties might include ensuring high accuracy and productivity rates.

EARNINGS

According to OfficeTeam's *2002 Salary Guide,* salaries for data entry specialists ranged from $19,500 to $23,500. The survey also found that senior data entry specialists earned between $22,000 and $26,000 per year.

The median annual income for data entry clerks in 2002 was $22,390, according to the U.S. Department of Labor. The Department also reported that, at the low end of the scale, 10 percent of data entry workers earned $15,910 or less. The highest paid 10 percent earned $26,840 or more. Salaries for these workers can vary depending on their employer, the complexity of their job duties, and their level of training. In addition, incomes tend to vary by region. Salaries for federal and local government employees are comparable to those in the private sector. Full-time and some part-time employees can expect benefits such as medical insurance, sick leave, and paid vacation.

WORK ENVIRONMENT

Most data entry clerks work 37–40 hours per week, with part-time positions becoming increasingly popular. Data entry workstations are usually located in comfortable, well-lighted areas. Data entry clerks must be able to work side by side with other employees and, in most cases, under close supervision. The work is routine, repetitive, and fast-paced and demands the constant, concentrated use of eyes and hands.

The continuous need for accuracy may be stressful to an individual unaccustomed to such working conditions. Duties may require lifting, reaching, and moving boxes of cards, tape, or other materials. Data entry personnel sit for long hours at a time. Long exposure to computer monitors at close range may strain the eyes, and constant use of the hands for typing may lead to nerve or muscle problems, such as carpal tunnel syndrome.

OUTLOOK

Because of improvements in data-processing technology that enable businesses to process greater volumes of information with fewer workers, the U.S. Department of Labor predicts that the employment outlook for data entry clerks is expected to decline through 2012. Jobs are becoming limited, for example, because many computer systems can now send information directly to another computer system without the need for a data entry clerk to input the information a second time. In addition, the widespread use of personal computers, which permit numerous employees to enter data directly, have also diminished the need for skilled entry personnel. Computer scanners, which read handwritten and typewritten information directly from source documents, and voice recognition technology are making data entry clerks obsolete. More businesses are also contracting temporary and staffing services or contracting data entry work out to overseas companies instead of hiring domestic full-time data entry clerks.

Even though there will be a slowdown in new job openings for data entry clerks, the high turnover rate due to current employees retiring or receiving job promotions will result in steady job opportunities. Those with the most advanced skills and the ability to adapt to the changing needs of the computer processing field will stand the best chance for continued employment. Job opportunities will be greatest in and around large metropolitan areas, where most banks, insurance and utilities companies, and government agencies are located.

Knowledge of different computer systems and general computer science enhances a data entry clerk's desirability for employers. The ability to work on different systems, particularly specialty systems such as page layout programs and typesetting programs, offers the clerk greater job flexibility.

FOR MORE INFORMATION

For more information on the data entry field, contact
Association for Computing Machinery
One Astor Plaza
1515 Broadway, 17th Floor
New York, NY 10036
Tel: 800-342-6626
Email: SIGS@acm.org
http://www.acm.org

For a brochure about careers in data processing and information about student chapters, contact
Association of Information Technology Professionals
401 North Michigan Avenue, Suite 2400
Chicago, IL 60611
Tel: 800-224-9371
http://www.aitp.org

Event Planners

OVERVIEW

The duties of *event planners* are varied and may include establishing a site for an event; making travel, hotel, and food arrangements; and planning the program and overseeing the registration. The planner may be responsible for all of the negotiating, planning, and coordinating for a major worldwide convention, or the planner may be involved with a small, in-house meeting involving only a few people. Some professional associations, government agencies, nonprofit organizations, political groups, and educational institutions hire event planners or have employees on staff who have these responsibilities. Many of these organizations and companies outsource their event-planning responsibilities to firms that specialize in these services, such as marketing, public relations, and event-planning firms. In addition, many event and meeting planners are independent consultants.

Some event planners' services are also used on a personal level to plan class or family reunions, birthday parties, weddings, or anniversaries. There are approximately 37,000 event planners employed in the United States.

HISTORY

According to the *National Directory of Occupational Titles and Codes,* the meeting-management profession was recognized as a career in the early 1990s. As corporations have specialized and expanded their companies to include facilities and employees worldwide, company meeting logistics have become more complex. Planning a meeting that brings together employees and directors from around the world requires advanced planning to acquire a site, make travel and hotel arrangements, book speakers and entertainment, and arrange for catering.

Similarly, the growth of the convention and trade show industry has resulted in the need for persons with skills specific to the planning, marketing, and execution of a successful show. Conventions, trade shows, meetings, and corporate travel have become a big business in recent years, accounting for approximately $80 billion in annual spending.

The scope of meetings has changed as well. Technological advances now allow meetings to be conducted via the Internet, through videoconferencing or closed circuit television, or by setting up conference calls.

THE JOB

Event planners have a variety of duties depending on their specific title and the firm they work for or the firms they work with. Generally, planners organize and plan an event such as a meeting, a special open house, a convention, or a specific celebration.

Meetings might consist of a small inter-department meeting, a board meeting, an all-employee meeting, an in-house training session, a stockholders' meeting, or a meeting with vendors or distributors. When planning for these events, meeting planners usually check the calendars of key executives to establish a meeting time that fits into their schedules. Planners reserve meeting rooms, training rooms, or outside facilities for the event. They visit outside sites to make sure they are appropriate for that specific event. Planners notify people of the time, place, and date of the event and set up registration procedures, if necessary. They arrange for food, room layout, audiovisual equipment, instructors, computers, sound equipment, and telephone equipment as required.

In some cases, a company may employ an in-house meeting planner who is responsible for small- to medium-sized events. When a large meeting, trade show, conference, open house, or convention is planned, the in-house event planner may contract with outside meeting planners to assist with specific responsibilities such as registration, catering, and display setup. Some companies have their own trade show or convention managers on staff.

Convention, trade show, or conference managers negotiate and communicate with other enterprises related to the convention or trade show industry such as hotel and catering sales staff, speaker's bureaus, and trade staff such as *electricians* or *laborers* who set up convention display areas. They may also be responsible for contracting the transportation of the equipment and supplies to and from the event site. The manager usually works with an established budget and negotiates fees with these enterprises and enters into contracts with them. Additional contracts may also need to be negotiated with professionals to handle registration, marketing, and public relations for the event.

Managers and planners need to be aware of legal aspects of trade show setups such as fire code regulations, floor plans, and space limitations, and make sure they are within these guidelines. They often need to get these arrangements approved in writing. Good record keeping and communication skills are used daily. The convention manager may have staff to handle the sales, registration, marketing, logistics, or other specific aspects of the event, or these duties may be subcontracted to another firm.

Some convention planners are employed specifically by convention and visitors' bureaus, the tourism industry, or by exhibit halls or convention facilities. Their job responsibilities may be specific to one aspect of the show, or they may be required to do any or all of the above-mentioned duties. Some convention and trade show managers may work for the exposition center or association and be responsible for selling booth space at large events.

Special-event coordinators are usually employed by large corporations who hold numerous special events or by firms who contract their special event planning services to companies, associations, or religious, political, or educational groups. A special-event coordinator is responsible for planning, organizing, and implementing a special event such as an open house, an anniversary, the dedication of a new facility, a special promotion or sale, an ordination, a political rally, or a victory celebration. This coordinator works with the company or organization and determines the purpose of the special event, the type of celebration desired, the site, the budget, the attendees, the food and entertainment preferences, and the anticipated outcome. The special-event planner then coordinates the vendors and equipment necessary to successfully hold this event. The coordinator works closely with the client at all times to ensure that the event is being planned as expected. Follow-up assessment of the event is usually part of the services offered by the special event coordinator.

Party planners are often employed by individuals, families, or small companies to help them plan a small party for a special occasion. Many party planners are independent contractors who work out of their homes or are employees of small firms. Party planners may help plan weddings, birthdays, christenings, bar or bat mitzvahs, anniversaries, or other events. They may be responsible for the entire event including the invitations, catering, decorating, entertainment, serving, and cleanup, or planners may simply perform one or two aspects such as contracting with a magician for a children's birthday party, recommending a menu, or greeting and serving guests.

REQUIREMENTS

High School

If you are interested in entering the field of event planning, you should take high school classes in business, English, and speech. Because many conferences and meetings are international in scope, you may also want to take foreign language and geography courses. In addition, computer science classes will be beneficial.

Postsecondary Training

Almost all coordinators and planners must have a four-year college degree to work for a company, corporation, convention, or travel center. Some institutions offer bachelor's degrees in meeting planning; however, degrees in business, English, communications, marketing, public relations, sales, or travel would also be a good fit for a career as a meetings manager, convention planner, or special-event coordinator. Many directors and planners who become company heads have earned graduate degrees.

Some small firms, convention centers, or exhibit facilities may accept persons with associate degrees or travel industry certification for certain planning positions. Party planners may not always need education beyond high school, but advancement opportunities will be more plentiful with additional education.

Certification or Licensing

There are some professional associations for planners that offer certification programs. For example, Meeting Professionals International offers the certification in meeting management designation. The International Association for Exhibition Management offers the certified in exhibition management designation. (See "For More Information" at the end of this article for contact information.)

Other Requirements

To be an event planner, you must have excellent organizational skills, the ability to plan projects and events, and the ability to think creatively. You must be able to work well with people and anticipate their needs in advance. You should be willing to pitch in to get a job done even though it may not be part of your duties. In a situation where there is an unforeseen crisis, you need to react quickly and professionally. Planners should have good negotiating and communication skills and be assertive but tactful.

EXPLORING

High school guidance counselors can supply information on event planners or convention coordinators. Public and school librarians may also be able to provide useful books, magazines, and pamphlets. Searching the Internet for companies that provide event-planning services can give you an idea of the types of services that they offer. Professional associations related to the travel, convention, and meeting industries may have career information available to students. Some of these organizations are listed at the end of this article.

Attending local trade shows and conventions will provide insight into the operations of this industry. Also, some exhibit and convention halls may hire students to assist with various aspects of trade show operations. You can learn more about this profession by subscribing to magazines such as *Meetings & Conventions* (http://www. meetings-conventions.com).

Some party planners may hire assistants to help with children's birthday parties or other special events. Organize and plan a large family event, such as a birthday, anniversary, graduation, or retirement celebration. You will have to find a location, hire catering or assign family members to bring specific food items, send invitations, purchase and arrange decorations, and organize entertainment, all according to what your budget allows.

You can also gain business experience through school activities. Join the business club, run for student council, or head up the prom committee to learn how to plan and carry out events.

EMPLOYERS

Many large corporations or institutions worldwide hire meeting managers, convention managers, or event planners to handle their specific activities. Although some companies may not have employees with the specific title of event planner or meeting manager, these skills are very marketable and these duties may be part of another job title. In many companies, these duties may be part of a position within the marketing, public relations, or corporate communications department.

Convention facilities, exhibit halls, training and educational institutions, travel companies, and health care facilities also hire event planners. Hotels often hire planners to handle meetings and events held within their facilities. Large associations usually maintain an event-planning staff for one or more annual conventions or business meetings for their members.

Job opportunities are also available with companies that contract out event and meeting planning services. Many of these companies have positions that specialize in certain aspects of the planning service, such as travel coordinator, exhibit planner, facilities negotiator, or they have people who perform specific functions such as trade show display setup, registration, and follow-up reporting.

Planners interested in jobs with the convention and trade show industries or hotels may find that larger cities have more demand for planners and offer higher salaries.

Experienced meeting planners or convention managers may choose to establish their own businesses or independently contract out their services. Party planning may also be a good independent business venture. Approximately 37,000 event planners are employed in the United States.

STARTING OUT

An internship at a visitors and convention bureau, exhibit center, or with a travel agency or meeting planning company is a good way to meet and network with other people in this field. Attending trade shows might offer a chance to speak with people about the field and to discuss any contacts they might have.

Some colleges and universities may offer job placement for people seeking careers in meeting planning or in the convention and trade show industries. Professional associations related to these industries are also good contacts for someone starting out. Classified ads and trade magazines may also offer some job leads.

ADVANCEMENT

Advancement opportunities for people in the event-planning field are good. Experienced planners can expect to move into positions of increased responsibility. They may become senior managers and executive directors of private businesses, hotels, convention facilities, exhibit halls, travel corporations, museums, or other facilities. They can advance within a corporation to a position with more responsibilities or they may go into the planning business for themselves. Planners who have established a good reputation in the industry are often recruited by other firms or facilities and can advance their careers with these opportunities.

EARNINGS

Meeting Professionals International reports that in 2002, the average salary for U.S. corporate meeting planners was $60,714. Planners with less than three years of experience made average salaries of $42,000, while very experienced planners made more than $85,000 a year. In the Northeast, meeting planners earned an average $66,453; in the West, $61,924; in the Midwest, $55,250; and in the South, $57,894.

Benefits may vary depending on the position and the employer but generally include vacation, sick leave, insurance, and other work-related benefits.

WORK ENVIRONMENT

Work environments vary with the planner's title and job responsibilities, but generally planners can expect to work in a business setting as part of a team. Usually, the planner's initial planning work is done in a clean environment with modern equipment prior to the opening of a convention or trade show. Working in convention and trade show environments, however, can be noisy, crowded, and distracting. In addition, the days can be long and may require standing for hours. If the planner is involved with supervising the setup or dismantling of a trade show or convention, the work can be dirty and physically demanding.

Although most facilities have crews that assist with setup, meeting planners occasionally get involved with last-minute changes and may need to do some physical lifting of equipment, tables, or chairs.

Event planners can usually expect to work erratic hours, often putting in long days prior to the event and the day the event is actually held. Travel is often part of the job requirements and may include working and/or traveling nights and weekends.

OUTLOOK

Job opportunities for event planners will continue to grow at a faster-than-average rate. The introduction of new technology enables more meetings to take place than ever before. Conventions, trade shows, meetings, and incentive travel support more than 1.5 million American jobs, according to the Professional Convention Management

Association (PCMA). These events account for more than $80 billion in annual spending.

FOR MORE INFORMATION

For information on careers in the field of event planning, contact the following organizations.

International Association for Exposition Management
8111 LBJ Freeway, Suite 750
Dallas, TX 75251
Tel: 972-458-8002
http://www.iaem.org

Meeting Professionals International
4455 LBJ Freeway, Suite 1200
Dallas, TX 75244
Tel: 972-702-3000
http://www.mpiweb.org

Professional Convention Management Association
2301 South Lake Shore Drive, Suite 1001
Chicago, IL 60616
Tel: 312-423-7262
http://www.pcma.org

―――――――――― **INTERVIEW** ――――――――――

Darrell Sparkman is a coordinator in the education and programs division of the industry leader in association and professional society management. In conjunction with other departments, he helps to plan and execute conferences for trade associations, professional societies, and technology user groups around the world. He spoke with the editors of Careers in Focus: Business *about his experiences.*

Q. How did you first become involved with event planning?

A. I first became involved in event planning when I worked for a major health care association, where I took on minor roles for their two major annual conferences. I wanted to expand upon this experience and go further into the continuing education field, and in a way that incorporated event planning. Next I worked for a company in their continuing education division, where I planned and implemented lectures, workshops, and courses. In my present position I am able to incorporate my desire to work in higher learning, while at the same time use my experience planning meetings and conferences. It's the best of both worlds for me.

Q. What are your main responsibilities on the job?

A. My main responsibility is to work with our volunteers and committees to set up the educational component of our conferences. People attend conferences for various reasons, but one important reason is that they want to expand their knowledge of their career, especially as it relates to their employer's business. I help recruit speakers and lecturers for educational sessions and workshops. I also work on the administrative side with committees and volunteers who provide the specific content of the educational tracks. Working with the volunteers is what really makes our conferences happen.

Q. What type of training and education did you pursue to work in this field? Did you complete any internships to prepare for your career?

A. I remember when I was in college a lot of people used to tell me that you never know what you may end up doing in life. So many people choose fields or careers that do not specifically relate to what they study, and that has somewhat been the case for me. I studied communication arts and public relations, specifically as they relate to arts administration. Even though I am not involved in arts administration now, I think my studies provided me with the skills that my job requires. I really enjoy what I do, so it just goes to show that you really do never know what you will end up doing!

Q. What would you say are the pros and cons of your job?

A. The travel involved with my job is definitely a pro. Event planning often involves travel. We plan conferences all over the world, and they can happen in some very interesting places. Another pro for me is the teamwork involved in what I do. Putting on a conference requires the talents of a lot of people—both within the company and with the client volunteers.

I think one con would be the uncertainty of what could happen during a conference. You never know what problems or issues might come up, and as much as you try to prepare for the unknown, there will be surprises. A lot of what I do requires patience and the ability to deal with these unanticipated events. That can be stressful sometimes.

Q. What would you say are the most important skills and personal qualities for someone in your field?

A. Someone involved in this field must have extremely good organizational skills and be very detail oriented. It's also important to be able to juggle a lot of projects at one time. I think people who work in this field enjoy working with people and being part of a team. I also think that people in this field enjoy a good challenge.

Q. How would someone starting out go about finding work in this field?

A. Probably the best way to start working in this field is to do an internship. Internships are the best way to get your foot in the door, because you can't always count on "falling" into something.

Q. What advice would you give to someone who is interested in pursuing this type of career?

A. Become involved in as many extracurricular activities as possible while in school, taking on leadership roles whenever possible. This will help set the stage for a career in event planning, because event planners are leaders who are required to make lots of decisions on a daily basis. School activities will help you learn more about people, specifically, how to deal with the various personalities you will encounter as an event planner.

Executive Recruiters

OVERVIEW

Executive recruiters are hired by businesses to locate, research, and interview candidates for hard-to-fill employment positions, mainly on the junior to senior management level. Such recruiters work for executive search firms and are paid by clients on a commission basis, or flat fee. There are approximately 10,000 executive recruiters employed by search firms located throughout the United States.

HISTORY

Although most companies have competent in-house human resource departments, a search for a top management position is often lengthy and difficult. Many times, human resource departments are not able to reach, or identify, the most qualified candidates. Also, a measure of privacy is lost if an entire department is aware of the need for a replacement. Companies are increasingly turning to a third party—the executive recruiter—for their employment needs.

Executive search firms fall into one of two categories: retained or contingency. *Retainer recruiters* work with upper-level management positions, such as CEOs or CFOs, with salary expectations averaging $150,000 or higher. They are exclusively contracted by a company or other entity to bring new executives on board. Retainer recruiters work on a flat-fee basis, or more commonly, for a percentage of the candidate's first-year salary and bonus. Commission percentages can range anywhere from 10 to 35 percent, although the industry standard is about a third of the candidate's proposed salary package. Executive recruiters, because of the high level

QUICK FACTS

School Subjects
Business
Psychology
Speech

Personal Skills
Communication/ideas
Leadership/management

Work Environment
Primarily indoors
Primarily multiple locations

Minimum Education Level
Bachelor's degree

Salary Range
$50,000 to $175,000 to
$250,000+

Certification or Licensing
None available

Outlook
Faster than the average

DOT
166

GOE
N/A

NOC
N/A

O*NET-SOC
13-1071.02

management positions they are assigned to fill and the exclusivity of their contract, usually take longer to complete their task—anywhere from three to six months, or more. The more qualities the company is looking for in a candidate, the longer the search.

The *contingency recruiter* deals with junior- to mid-level executive positions paying $50,000 to $150,000. Such recruiters are paid only if the candidate they present is hired for the job; pay is usually a percentage of the first-year salary package. Many times, however, a company will have more than one contingency firm working to fill a single position. Because of this, contingency recruiters are not guaranteed a fee and they may spend less time on their search. Some contingency recruiters also charge on an hourly basis or may work for a flat fee.

THE JOB

Most companies—from *Fortune 500* firms to colleges and universities to small businesses—at one time or another have come across the need to replace an important executive or administrator. Because of restraints such as time, privacy, or resources, many businesses opt to use the services of an executive recruiter. The task begins once the search firm is retained (notified of the job opening) and is asked to find the best possible candidate.

The recruiter first evaluates the needs and structure of the company and the specifications of the open position. Then a written draft of the job description is made, detailing the title, job definition, responsibilities, and compensation. At this time, a wish list is composed of every possible quality, talent, skill, and educational background the perfect job candidate should possess. It is up to the recruiter to match these specifications as closely as possible.

Once a written contract is approved by the client, then the real work begins. The three traditional job functions in the recruitment industry are: researcher, associate, and consultant. *Researchers* conduct research to find possible candidates. They look through directories and databases, and network with contacts familiar with the field. They read trade papers and magazines as well as national newspapers such as the *Wall Street Journal* and the *New York Times*. Business sections of newspapers often include write-ups of industry leaders. Recruiters also receive resumes from people looking to change employment, which they may use for future reference. It's imperative recruiters stay current with the field they specialize in; they need to be familiar with the key players as well as important technological advances that may change the scope of the industry.

Ethics in Recruiting

Trust and confidentiality are major issues in executive recruiting. In their search to fill top-level executive positions, recruiters are trusted with confidential corporate and personal information. Clients must be able to trust that the recruiter will choose candidates fairly and objectively. The National Association of Executive Recruiters requires the following of all its members to ensure objective and accurate recruiting practices:

- Clients, positions, and candidates must be represented honestly and factually.

- Members shall honor the confidentiality of proprietary information received from clients and candidates.

- Members shall conduct reference checks of all candidates prior to final selection.

- Members shall refrain from soliciting candidates from client companies.

- Members shall inform clients of potential limitations that might affect the outcome of their search.

- Members shall not accept payment for counseling or other assistance to individuals seeking employment.

Once a long list is assembled, *associates* contact the prospective candidates, usually by telephone. Candidates who are interested and qualified are screened further; references are checked fully. *Consultants* conduct personal interviews with promising candidates who make the short list of hopefuls. Consultants also manage client relationships and develop new business for the firm.

The goal of retainer executive recruiters is to present three to five of the best candidates to a client for final interviews. Contingency recruiters, on the other hand, will present many qualified candidates to the client, to better their chance of filling the position. Executive recruiters will not edit resumes or coach on the interview process, but some will offer information on where candidates stand after the initial interview and give advice on strengths and perceived weaknesses.

A search for the perfect executive is a lengthy process. Most searches take anywhere from one month to a year or more. Once the position is filled, recruiters conduct one or more follow-ups to make sure the employee's transition into the company is smooth. Any conflicts or discrepancies are addressed and often mediated by, or along with, the search firm. Some executive search firms offer some kind of guarantee with their work. If the hired employee leaves a firm within a specified period of time or does not work out as anticipated, then the recruiter will find a replacement for a reduced fee or at no charge.

REQUIREMENTS

High School
To prepare for a career as an executive recruiter, you should take business, speech, English, and mathematics classes in high school. Psychology and sociology courses will teach you how to recognize personality characteristics that may be key in helping you determine which job candidates would best fit a position.

Postsecondary Training
You will need at least a bachelor's degree and several years of work experience to become an executive recruiter. Postsecondary courses helpful to this career include communications, marketing, and business administration. Some colleges offer undergraduate degrees in human resources management or business degrees with a concentration in human resources management. To have more job opportunities, you may also consider getting a master's degree in one of these fields. Most recruiters move into this industry after successful careers in their particular areas of expertise (for example, health care, finance, publishing, or computers) and they come to the field with a variety of educational backgrounds.

Certification or Licensing
There are no certification or licensing requirements for this industry. Most executive search professionals belong to the Association of Executive Search Consultants or the National Association of Executive Recruiters.

Other Requirements
Executive recruiters need strong people skills. Good communicators are in demand, especially those who can maintain a high level of integrity and confidentiality. Recruiters are privy to sensitive company and employee information that may prove disastrous if leaked to the public.

An executive recruiter conducts an interview with a job candidate.
(Getty Images)

The most powerful tool in this industry is a network of good contacts. Since executive recruiters come on board after working in the field for which they are now recruiting, they are usually familiar with who's who in the business.

EXPLORING

Familiarize yourself with business practices by joining or starting a business club at your school. Being a part of a speech or debate team is a great way to develop excellent speaking skills, which are necessary in this field. Hold mock interviews with family or friends, and get work and volunteer experience in your specialized field (for example, health care or publishing). Professional associations, such as The International Association of Corporate and Professional Recruiters, are also good sources of information. Visit this association's website (http://www.iacpr.org) to learn more.

EMPLOYERS

Executive search firms of all sizes are located throughout the United States. Most specialize in placement in a particular field, for example, chemical engineering or advertising. For a list of search firms, you may want to refer to the *Directory of Executive Recruiters,* also known in the industry as the "Red Book." Search firms in the United States employ approximately 10,000 executive recruiters, according to an estimate by *Executive Recruiter News.*

STARTING OUT

A common starting point in this industry is a position at a contingency search firm, or even an outplacement center. Responsibilities may be limited at first, but a successful and consistent track record should lead to bigger clients, more placements, and higher commissions. Many executive recruiters were recruited into the field themselves, especially if they were well known in their industry. It is important to market yourself and your accomplishments while you work in entry-level positions. Circulate among the movers and shakers of your company, as well as those of the competition. They may prove to be valuable contacts for the future. Most importantly, cultivate relationships with any recruitment firms that may call; you'll never know when their assistance may be desired, or necessary.

ADVANCEMENT

A typical advancement path in this industry would be a transfer to a retainer-based search firm. Retained search firms deal with the upper-echelon administrative positions that pay top salaries, translating to higher commissions for the recruiter.

Let's say you've already paid your dues and worked successfully at a retainer search firm. What next? You may want to negotiate for partnership or opt to call the shots and start a firm of your own.

EARNINGS

Executive recruiters are paid well for their efforts. Contingency recruiters, who get paid only if their candidate is hired, typically charge a fee from 25 percent to 35 percent of the candidate's first-year cash compensation.

Retained recruiters average fees of one-third of the candidate's first-year cash compensation. The employer usually pays any expenses incurred by the recruiter. According to *U.S. News & World Report,* average entry-level positions pay from $50,000 to $100,000 annually, while mid-level recruiters earn from $100,000 to $250,000. Top earners, those working for larger retainer recruiting firms, can make more than $250,000 a year. Along with their salary, all recruiters are offered a benefit package including health insurance, paid vacations, and sick time or paid disability.

WORK ENVIRONMENT

Many recruiters work 50–70 hours a week; it's not uncommon for recruiters to spend several days a week on the road meeting clients, interviewing, or doing candidate research. Also, aspiring recruiters should expect to spend most of their day on the phone.

OUTLOOK

The executive search industry should have a good future. Potential clients include not only large international corporations but also universities, the government, and smaller businesses. Smaller operations are aware that having a solid executive or administrator may make the difference between turning a profit or not being in business at all. Many times, search firm services are used to conduct industry research or to scope out the competition. Executive search firms now specialize in many fields of employment—health care, engineering, or accounting, for example.

The era of company loyalty and employment for life is over in the corporate world. Many savvy workers campaign aggressively and will transfer given a larger salary, improved benefits, and stock options—in short, a better employment future. Employers, on the other hand, realize the importance in having qualified and experienced employees at the helm of their business. Most companies are willing to pay the price, whether a retainer fee or commission, to find just the right person for the job.

According to the Association of Executive Search Consultants, it is becoming more important for executive recruiters to operate on a global basis. They must be able to conduct searches for clients and candidates in other countries. Peter Felix, president of AESC, says, "Today, the retained executive search business is a $10 billion industry operating in all the major economies of the world. In this era of the knowledge society where executive talent is so important, executive search is seen increasingly as a critical management tool."

FOR MORE INFORMATION

For industry information, contact
The Association of Executive Search Consultants
500 Fifth Avenue, Suite 930
New York, NY 10110-0900
Tel: 212-398-9556
Email: aesc@aesc.org
http://www.aesc.org

For more industry information, or membership information, contact
National Association of Executive Recruiters
1320 Tower Road
Schaumburg, IL 60173
Tel: 847-598-3680
http://www.naer.org

For a copy of the industry newsletter Executive Recruiter News or the Directory of Executive Recruiters, *contact*
Kennedy Information
One Phoenix Mill Lane, 5th Floor
Peterborough, NH 03458
Tel: 800-531-0007
Email: bookstore@kennedyinfo.com
http://www.kennedyinfo.com

Labor Union Business Agents

OVERVIEW

Labor union business agents manage the daily business matters of labor unions and act as liaisons between the union and management during contract negotiations. They manage business affairs for the labor union that employs them and inform the media of labor union happenings. Labor union business agents are also responsible for informing employers of workers' concerns.

HISTORY

The idea of workers or craft workers banding together for their mutual benefit has existed for centuries. In the Middle Ages, groups such as blacksmiths and carpenters organized themselves into guilds, which established product and wage standards, set requirements for entering the trade, and erected barriers to outside competition. The first guilds in the United States were organized around the time of the Revolutionary War.

Unions were first organized in both England and the United States by workers in response to the industrial revolution of the 19th century. In 1886, the American Federation of Labor (AFL) was founded. Through collective bargaining tactics, the AFL was able to get higher wages, shorter hours, workers' compensation, and child labor laws. In the beginning of the 20th century, there was a huge growth in union membership, which jumped from less than 800,000 in 1900 to more than 5 million by 1920. Unionism got a further boost from such New Deal federal

QUICK FACTS

School Subjects
Business
English
Mathematics

Personal Skills
Communication/ideas
Leadership/management

Work Environment
Indoors and outdoors
Primarily multiple locations

Minimum Education Level
High school diploma

Salary Range
$50,000 to $65,000 to $75,000+

Certification or Licensing
None available

Outlook
About as fast as the average

DOT
187

GOE
11.05.02

NOC
1121

O*NET-SOC
N/A

legislation as the Wagner Act in 1935, which established the National Labor Relations Board. In the same year, the Congress of Industrial Organizations (CIO) was created to bring about a separation between unions representing factory workers and those representing skilled craftsmen. The two groups eventually merged together forming the AFL-CIO, which still exerts a powerful influence on improving working relations today.

Most unions are essentially organized into two types: the *craft union*, whose members are all skilled in a certain craft, such as carpentry or electrical work; and the *industrial union*, whose members work in the various jobs of a certain industry, such as automobiles or steel manufacturing. Companies began to reorganize around the existence of unions. A company that hired only union members was called a *closed shop*, while a *union shop* was one that required newly hired workers to join a union after a certain time period. The closed shop was outlawed in 1947 with the passage of the Taft-Hartley Act. Since then, more than one-third of the states have also outlawed the union shop by passing "right to work" laws.

The economic recession in the early 1980s caused a weakening of many unions' power, as employers in financially troubled industries asked unions for contract concessions in order to save the jobs of existing employees. In 2000, 13.5 percent of wage and salary workers were represented by unions, according to the U.S. Department of Labor.

THE JOB

Union business agents act as representatives for the working members of the union, who are often called the "rank and file." Agents are usually elected by members in a democratic fashion, although sometimes they are appointed by the union's elected officers or executive board. A union agent normally represents a certain number of workers. In an industrial union, an agent could speak for workers in several small plants or a single large plant. In a craft union, an agent will represent a single trade or group of craft workers.

Unions are structured like corporations and government groups in many ways. In the same way that a company will follow the procedures described in its articles of incorporation to conduct meetings and elect its board of directors, a union follows the rules set down by its own constitution and democratically elects its leaders and representatives. Union leaders must be responsive to the wills of their union members, or they may be overruled in union meetings or defeated in their next bid for reelection. In industrial unions, local chapters are directed by a central union, which is led by a regional director and is part of a larger national or international union.

Craft unions are organized somewhat differently. Each craft is represented by a different business agent, and several of these agents work on the staff of a district council. These district councils are like an organization of unions, each governed independently of the others, banding together for bargaining strength.

One of the most important aspects of a union business agent's job is the role as a liaison, or go-between, for workers and employers. This role becomes most apparent at the times when the union and its employers need to negotiate a new contract. The business agent needs to know what the members of the union want in order to talk with management about wages, benefits, pensions, working conditions, layoffs, workers' compensation, and other issues. The agent explains the union's position to management during prebargaining talks. During negotiations, the agent keeps the members informed of the progress of contract talks and advises them of management's position.

The business agent needs to be able to drive a hard bargain with employers while at the same time be aware of employer limitations so that an agreement can be reached suitable to all parties. If a contract agreement cannot be reached, a third party may be needed. *Conciliators,* or *mediators,* are dispute-resolution specialists that may be brought in to keep the talks moving on both sides. *Arbitrators,* sometimes called *referees* or *umpires,* help decide disputes by drawing up conditions that bind both workers and employers to certain agreements. Only as a last resort will labor union business agents help organize a general strike, which can hurt both labor and management financially. During a strike, workers are not paid and employers lose money from a loss in production.

In addition, the business agent is responsible for making certain that the union is serving its members properly. The agent often handles grievances expressed by union members and, if necessary, will work with people in the company to solve them. It is also the agent's job to make sure that employers carry out the terms of the union's contract. The agent is in constant contact with union members through the *shop steward,* who is the general representative for the union. The steward is either elected by the membership or appointed by the business agent.

Agents are also responsible for much of the public image of the union. This involves everything from contacting newspaper reporters and other members of the media to organizing charity drives. The business agent is often in charge of recruiting new members for the union, finding jobs for members who are out of work, conducting union meetings, and renting meeting halls.

REQUIREMENTS

High School
Union business agents should at least have a high school education. To build a solid background, take courses in business, English, mathematics, public speaking, history, and economics. If available, you should also take technical courses, such as shop and electronics.

Postsecondary Training
A college degree can also be very valuable for union business agents. Many colleges now offer curricula in labor and industrial relations. Additional courses that you will also find useful include psychology, business, collective bargaining, labor law, occupational safety and health, economics, and political science. Some unions may offer to reimburse some of the costs of higher education for union members interested in leadership positions. In most cases, business agents will receive additional training on the job while working under experienced union leaders.

Other Requirements
To succeed as a union business agent, you need to have both relevant job skills and leadership qualities. Agents should have previous work experience in the trade, industry, or profession in which they represent in order to fully understand and appreciate the problems and concerns of the workers. Most business agents begin as industrial or craft workers, join a union, become involved in its affairs, and progressively move up through the ranks.

Agents must also possess leadership skills and be committed to the cause of the union and to the rights and concerns of the workers. Their role in negotiations requires intelligence, persuasiveness, self-discipline, and patience. They must be able to command the respect of both the employer and the members. A good command of the English language, both written and oral, is essential to vocalize the concerns of the workers, understand the terms of union contracts, and persuade the representatives of the company and the union members to accept an agreement. If the union leadership has reached a decision that may be unpopular, the agent will have to explain the reasoning behind it to the members.

EXPLORING

The career of labor union business agent offers you the opportunity to follow your career interest into such fields as teaching or electronics, and then expand as a leader of others. Whatever your specific interest area, you should also gain experience in policy making and hold positions of leadership to nurture the qualities necessary for a future career as a union business agent. Get involved with the student council, debate society, and other clubs with leadership opportunities. In addition, talking with working business agents can also lend insight into the daily responsibilities of union leadership.

EMPLOYERS

Since union business agents represent the workers in a labor union, they are employed by the various craft and industrial unions that normally represent a particular group of workers. There are active unions in nearly every line of work.

STARTING OUT

Almost all union business agents first work for a number of years in their respective industries and work their way up from the inside. Each type of industry has its own requirements for joining, such as previous experience, training, and apprenticeships. Once a member of a union, workers can seek out opportunities to become involved in union matters, such as serving on committees. Through efforts and dedication to the union's cause, workers attract the attention of union leadership, who may encourage them to run for a local union job in the next election. Initially, prospective agents are usually elected or appointed to the position of shop steward, who is responsible for communicating the members' wishes to the business agent. If popular and effective, the steward may then run for election as a union business agent. The process of electing or selecting representatives varies from union to union, but an agent usually serves a term of about three years.

ADVANCEMENT

A labor union business agent is in many ways like a politician. In the same ways that politicians can work their way from local to state government and possibly to Washington, D.C., union business agents can move upward in the ranks of leadership. If business agents do their jobs well, gain respect, and maintain high profiles, they may advance to positions at the council headquarters or at regional union offices. An experienced agent can even advance to represent the union at the international level.

EARNINGS

The earnings of business agents vary depending on the union's membership size and the type of business it represents. Agents' pay is usually prescribed in union bylaws or its constitution. Typically, their wages mirror the earnings of the highest-paid worker in the particular field the agent represents. Average starting salaries for agents are about $50,000. After five years' experience, business agents earn about $65,000, and after 10 years, $75,000 or more.

In addition, agents get the same benefits as other union members, such as paid holidays, health insurance, and pension plans. Some agents may drive a car owned by the union and have their expenses paid while they travel on union business.

WORK ENVIRONMENT

An agent's dedication to the union often dictates the amount of hours worked every week. Most agents work a 40-hour week, but often work much longer hours during contract bargaining talks and membership drives. They are also expected to be available 24 hours a day to handle any possible emergencies.

Agents generally split their time between office work at council or local headquarters, and fieldwork. They spend many hours visiting factories and construction sites, meeting with shop stewards, and listening to the opinions of the rank-and-file members. During these visits, they have to deal with the working conditions of their industry. Agents also travel a great deal and can be on the road for long periods of time.

OUTLOOK

The success of union business agents depends to a great extent on the strength and growth prospects of their particular unions as well as of their industries in general. The best opportunities for employment and advancement exist in those industries that are expected to grow in years to come.

In recent years, there has been a strong shift in the U.S. economy away from manufacturing toward service industries. Such service industries include insurance, banking, legal services, health care, accounting, retailing, data processing, and education. According to the U.S. Department of Labor, the growth of these industries and the industries that support them will provide the greatest opportunities for unionization and union business agents through 2012. Unions already exist for public workers, such as teachers, police officers, and firefighters. Other opportunities for unionization and business agent employment will arise in health care, representing workers such as physicians, nurses, medical assistants, technicians, and custodians.

The manufacturing sector of the economy, which traditionally has been very highly unionized, is expected to lose jobs because of increasingly efficient technologies and competition from overseas. However, certain areas of opportunity will still exist in manufacturing. Increases are expected in certain durable goods industries, such as computing equipment, medical supplies, plastics, and commercial printing. Construction is the only goods-producing sector of the economy that is expected to show a steady increase in employment in the next decade.

FOR MORE INFORMATION

Following are a handful of national labor unions. For more detailed information about careers in a specific trade or profession, contact the appropriate local unions in your area.

American Federation of Labor and Congress of Industrial
  Organizations
815 16th Street, NW
Washington, DC 20006
Tel: 202-637-5000
Email: feedback@aflcio.org
http://www.aflcio.org

American Federation of Teachers
555 New Jersey Avenue, NW
Washington, DC 20001
Tel: 202-879-4400
Email: online@aft.org
http://www.aft.org

International Union, United Automobile, Aerospace and Agricultural Implement Workers of America
8000 East Jefferson Avenue
Detroit, MI 48214
Tel: 313-926-5000
Email: uaw@uaw.org
http://www.uaw.org

United Steelworkers of America
Five Gateway Center
Pittsburgh, PA 15222
Tel: 412-562-2400
http://www.uswa.org

Management Analysts and Consultants

OVERVIEW

Management analysts and consultants analyze business or operating procedures to devise the most efficient methods of accomplishing work. They gather and organize information about operating problems and procedures and prepare recommendations for implementing new systems or changes. They may update manuals outlining established methods of performing work and train personnel in new applications. There are approximately 577,000 management analysts and consultants employed in the United States.

HISTORY

A number of people in business began experimenting with accepted management practices after the industrial revolution. For example, in the 1700s Josiah Wedgwood applied new labor- and work-saving methods to his pottery business and was the first to formulate the concept of mass-producing articles of uniform quality. He believed the manufacturing process could be organized into a system that would use, and not abuse, the people harnessed to it. He organized the interrelationships between people, material, and events in his factory and took the time to reflect upon them. In short, he did in the 18th century what management analysts and consultants do today.

Frederick W. Taylor was the creator of the "efficiency cult" in American business. Taylor invented the world-famous "differential piecework" plan, in which a productive worker could significantly increase take-home pay by stepping up the pace of work. Taylor's well-publicized study of the Midvale Steel plant in Pennsylvania was the first time-and-motion study. It broke down elements of each part of each job and timed it, and enabled Taylor to quantify maximum efficiency. He earned many assignments and inspired James O. McKinsey, in 1910, to found a firm dealing with management and accounting problems.

Today, management analysts and consultants are thriving. As technological advances lead to the possibility of dramatic loss or gain in the business world, many executives feel more secure relying on all the specialized expertise they can find.

THE JOB

Management analysts and consultants are called in to solve any of a vast array of organizational problems. They are often needed when a rapidly growing small company needs a better system of control over inventories and expenses.

The role of the consultant is to come into a situation in which a client is unsure or inexpert and to recommend actions or provide assessments. There are many different types of management analysts and consultants. In general, they all require knowledge of general management, operations, marketing, logistics, materials management and physical distribution, finance and accounting, human resources, electronic data processing and systems, and management science.

Management analysts and consultants may be called in when a major manufacturer must reorganize its corporate structure when acquiring a new division. For example, they assist when a company relocates to another state by coordinating the move, planning the new facility, and training new workers.

The work of management analysts and consultants is quite flexible—it varies from job to job. In general, management analysts and consultants collect, review, and analyze data, make recommendations, and assist in the implementation of their proposals. Some projects require several consultants to work together, each specializing in a different area. Other jobs require the analysts to work independently.

Public and private organizations use management analysts for a variety of reasons. Some organizations lack the resources necessary to handle a project. Other organizations, before they pursue a particular course of action, will consult an analyst to determine what resources will be required or what problems will be encountered. Some companies seek outside advice on how to resolve organizational problems that have already been identified or to avoid troublesome problems that could arise.

Firms providing consulting practitioners range in size from solo practitioners to large international companies employing hundreds of people. The services are generally provided on a contract basis. A company will choose a consulting firm that specializes in the area that needs assistance, and then the two firms negotiate the conditions of the contract. Contract variables include the proposed cost of the project, staffing requirements, and the deadline.

After getting a contract, the analyst's first job is to define the nature and extent of the project. He or she analyzes statistics, such as annual revenues, employment, or expenditures. He or she may also interview employees and observe the operations of the organization on a day-to-day basis.

The next step for the analyst is to use his or her knowledge of management systems to develop solutions. While preparing recommendations, he or she must take into account the general nature of the business, the relationship of the firm to others in its industry, the firm's internal organization, and the information gained through data collection and analysis.

Once they have decided on a course of action, management analysts and consultants usually write reports of their findings and recommendations and present them to the client. They often make formal oral presentations about their findings as well. Some projects require only reports; others require assistance in implementing the suggestions.

REQUIREMENTS
High School
High school courses that will give you a general preparation for this field include business, mathematics, and computer science. Management analysts and consultants must pass on their findings through written or oral presentations, so be sure to take English and speech classes, too.

Postsecondary Training
Employers generally prefer to hire management analysts and consultants with a master's degree in business or public administration, or at least a bachelor's degree and several years of appropriate work experience. Many college majors provide a suitable education for this occupation because of the diversity of problem areas addressed by management analysts and consultants. These include many areas in

the computer and information sciences, engineering, business and management, education, communications, marketing and distribution, and architecture and environmental design.

When hired directly from school, management analysts and consultants often participate in formal company training programs. These programs may include instruction on policies and procedures, computer systems and software, and management practices and principles. Regardless of their background, most management analysts and consultants routinely attend conferences to keep abreast of current developments in the field.

Certification and Licensing

The Institute of Management Consultants, in cooperation with the Association of Internal Management Consultants, Inc., offers the certified management consultant designation to those who pass an examination and interview and who meet minimum educational and experience criteria. Certification must be renewed every three years. Certification is voluntary, but may provide an additional advantage to job seekers.

Other Requirements

Management analysts and consultants are often responsible for recommending layoffs of staff, so it is important that they learn to deal with people diplomatically. Their job requires a great deal of tact, enlisting cooperation while exerting leadership, debating their points, and pointing out errors. Consultants must be quick thinkers, able to refute objections with finality. They also must be able to make excellent presentations.

A management analyst must also be unbiased and analytical, with a disposition toward the intellectual side of business and a natural curiosity about the way things work best.

EXPLORING

The reference departments of most libraries include business areas that will have valuable research tools such as encyclopedias of business consultants and "who's who" of business consultants. These books should list management analysis and consulting firms across the country, describing their annual sales and area of specialization, like industrial, high tech, small business, and retail. After doing some research, you can call or write to these firms and ask for more information.

For more general business exploration, see if your school has a business or young leaders club. If there is nothing of the sort, you may want to explore Junior Achievement, a nationwide association that connects young business-minded students with professionals in the field for mentoring and career advice. Visit http://www.ja.org for more information.

EMPLOYERS

About a third of all management analysts and consultants are self-employed. Federal, state, and local governments and science and technology consulting firms employ many of the others. The Department of Defense employs the majority of those working for the federal government. Although management analysts and consultants are found throughout the country, the majority are concentrated in major metropolitan areas.

STARTING OUT

Most government agencies offer entry-level analyst and consultant positions to people with bachelor's degrees and no work experience. Many entrants are also career changers who were formerly mid- and upper-level managers. With one-third of the practicing management consultants self-employed, career changing is a common route into the field.

Anyone with some degree of business expertise can begin to work as an independent consultant. The number of one- and two-person consulting firms in this country is well over 100,000. Establishing a wide range of appropriate personal contacts is by far the most effective way to get started in this field. Consultants have to sell themselves and their expertise, a task far tougher than selling a tangible product the customer can see and handle. Many consultants get their first clients by advertising in newspapers, magazines, and trade or professional periodicals. After some time in the field, word-of-mouth advertising is often the primary force.

ADVANCEMENT

A new consultant in a large firm may be referred to as an *associate* for the first couple of years. The next progression is to *senior associate,* a title that indicates three to five years' experience and the ability to supervise others and do more complex and independent work. After about five years, the analyst who is progressing well may become an *engagement manager* with the responsibility to lead a consulting team on a particular client project. The best managers become *senior engagement managers,* leading several study teams or a very large project team. After about seven years, those who excel will be considered for appointment as *junior partners* or *principals.* Partnership involves responsibility for marketing the firm and leading client projects. Some may be promoted to senior partnership or *director,* but few people successfully run this full course. Management analysts and consultants with entrepreneurial ambition may open their own firms.

EARNINGS

In 2002, management analysts and consultants had median annual earnings of $60,340, according to the Bureau of Labor Statistics. The lowest 10 percent earned less than $35,990 and the highest 10 percent earned more than $115,670.

Salaries and hourly rates for management analysts and consultants vary widely, according to experience, specialization, education, and employer. The *Occupational Outlook Handbook* reports that analysts and consultants employed by state governments earned median annual salaries of $47,340, while those working for management, scientific, and technical consulting services earned a median annual salary of $71,790.

Many consultants can demand between $400 and $1,000 per day. Their fees are often well over $40 per hour. Self-employed management consultants receive no fringe benefits and generally have to maintain their own office, but their pay is usually much higher than salaried consultants. They can make more than $2,000 per day or $250,000 in one year from consulting just two days per week.

Typical benefits for salaried analysts and consultants include health and life insurance, retirement plans, vacation and sick leave, profit sharing, and bonuses for outstanding work. The employer generally reimburses all travel expenses.

WORK ENVIRONMENT

Management analysts and consultants generally divide their time between their own offices and the client's office or production facility. They can spend a great deal of time on the road.

Most management analysts and consultants work at least 40 hours per week plus overtime depending on the project. The nature of consulting projects—working on location with a single client toward a specific goal—allows these professionals to totally immerse themselves in their work. They sometimes work 14–16-hour days, and six- or seven-day workweeks can be fairly common.

While self-employed, consultants may enjoy the luxury of setting their own hours and doing a great deal of their work at home; the trade-off is sacrificing the benefits provided by the large firms. Their livelihood depends on the additional responsibility of maintaining and expanding their clientele on their own.

Although those in this career usually avoid much of the potential tedium of working for one company all day, every day, they face many pressures resulting from deadlines and client expectations. Because the clients are generally paying generous fees, they want to see dramatic results, and the management analyst can feel the weight of this.

OUTLOOK

Employment of management analysts is expected to grow faster than the average for all occupations through 2012, according to the U.S. Department of Labor. Industry and government agencies are expected to rely more and more on the expertise of these professionals to improve and streamline the performance of their organizations. Job growth will also be strong in very large firms with an international focus and in smaller firms that specialize in areas such as health care, biotechnology, engineering, and marketing. Many job openings will result from the need to replace personnel who transfer to other fields or leave the labor force.

Competition for management consulting jobs will be strong. Employers can choose from a large pool of applicants who have a wide variety of educational backgrounds and experience. The challenging nature of this job, coupled with high salary potential, attracts many. A graduate degree, experience and expertise in the industry, as well as a knack for public relations, are needed to stay competitive.

Trends that have increased the growth of employment in this field include advancements in information technology and e-commerce, the growth of international business, and fluctuations in the economy that have forced businesses to streamline and downsize.

FOR MORE INFORMATION

For industry information, contact the following organizations:
American Management Association
1601 Broadway
New York, NY 10019
Tel: 800-262-9699
http://www.amanet.org

Association of Management Consulting Firms
380 Lexington Avenue, Suite 1700
New York, NY 10168
Tel: 212-551-7887
Email: info@amcf.org
http://www.amcf.org

For information on certification, contact
Association of Internal Management Consultants, Inc.
86 Clarendon Avenue
West Rutland, VT 05777
Tel: 802-438-2882
Email: info@aimc.org
http://aimc.org

For information on certification, contact
Institute of Management Consultants USA
2025 M Street, NW, Suite 800
Washington, DC 20036
Tel: 800-221-2557
Email: office@imcusa.org
http://www.imcusa.org

Office Administrators

OVERVIEW

Office administrators direct and coordinate the work activities of office workers within an office. They supervise office clerks and other workers in their tasks and plan department activities with other supervisory personnel. Administrators often define job duties and develop training programs for new workers. They evaluate the progress of their clerks and work with upper management officials to ensure that the office staff meets productivity and quality goals. Office administrators often meet with office personnel to discuss job-related issues or problems, and they are responsible for maintaining a positive office environment. There are approximately 1.5 million office administrators employed in the United States.

HISTORY

The growth of business since the industrial revolution has been accompanied by a corresponding growth in the amount of work done in offices. Records, bills, receipts, contracts, and other paperwork have proliferated. Phone calls, emails, and other communications have multiplied. Accounting and bookkeeping practices have become more complicated.

The role of the office administrator has also grown over time. In the past, such supervisors were responsible mainly for ensuring productivity and good work from their clerks and reporting information to management. Today, office administrators play a more active part in the operations of busy offices. They are responsible for coordinating the activities of many departments, informing management of departmental performance, and making sure the highly specialized sectors of an office run smoothly and efficiently every day.

THE JOB

As modern technology and an increased volume of business communications become a normal part of daily business, offices are becoming more complicated places in which to work. By directing and coordinating the activities of clerks and other office workers, office administrators are an integral part of an effective organization.

The day-to-day work of office administrators, also known as *office managers,* involves organizing and overseeing many different activities. Although specific duties vary with the type and size of the particular office, all supervisors and managers have several basic job responsibilities. The primary responsibility of the office administrator is to run the office; that is, whatever the nature of the office's business, the office administrator must see to it that all workers have what they need to do their work.

Office administrators are usually responsible for interviewing prospective employees and making recommendations on hiring. They train new workers, explain office policies, and explain performance criteria. Office administrators are also responsible for delegating work responsibilities. This requires a keen understanding of the strengths and weaknesses of each worker, as well as the ability to determine what needs to be done and when it must be completed. For example, if a supervisor knows that one worker is especially good at filing business correspondence, that person will probably be assigned important filing tasks. Office administrators often know how to do many of the tasks done by their subordinates and assist or relieve them whenever necessary.

Office administrators not only train clerical workers and assign them job duties but also recommend increases in salaries, promote workers when approved, and occasionally fire them. Therefore, they must carefully observe clerical workers performing their jobs (whether answering the telephones, opening and sorting mail, or inputting computer data) and make positive suggestions for any necessary improvements. Managers who can communicate effectively, both verbally and in writing, will be better able to carry out this kind of work. Motivating employees to do their best work is another important component of an office administrator's responsibilities.

Office administrators must be very good at human relations. Differences of opinion and personality clashes among employees are inevitable in almost any office, and the administrator must be able to deal with grievances and restore good feelings among the staff. Office administrators meet regularly with their staff, alone and in groups, to discuss and solve any problems that might affect people's job performance.

Planning is a vital and time-consuming portion of the job responsibilities of office administrators. Not only do they plan the work of subordinates, they also assist in planning current and future office space needs, work schedules, and the types of office equipment and supplies that need to be purchased.

Office administrators must always keep their superiors informed as to the overall situation in the clerical area. If there is a delay on an important project, for example, upper management must know the cause and the steps being taken to expedite the matter.

REQUIREMENTS

High School

A high school diploma is essential for this position, and a college degree is highly recommended. You should take courses in English, speech and communications, mathematics, sociology, history, and as many business-related courses, such as typing and bookkeeping, as possible. Knowledge of a wide variety of computer software programs is also very important.

Postsecondary Training

In college, pursue a degree in business administration or at least take several courses in business management and operations. In some cases, an associate's degree is considered sufficient for a supervisory position, but a bachelor's degree will make you more attractive to employers and help in advancement.

Many community colleges and vocational schools offer business education courses that help train office administrators. The American Management Association has a Self-Study Certificate Program in several areas, including customer service management, human resources management, general management, strategic leadership, and others. (See contact information at the end of this article.)

Colleges and universities nationwide offer bachelor's degrees in business administration; a few may offer programs targeted to specific industries, such as medical administration or hotel management.

Other Requirements

Offices can be hectic places. Deadlines on major projects can create tension, especially if some workers are sick or overburdened. Office administrators must constantly juggle the demands of their superiors with the capabilities of their subordinates. Thus, they need an even temperament and the ability to work well with others. Additional important attributes include organizational ability, attention to detail, dependability, and trustworthiness. Since many offices promote administrators from clerical work positions within their organization, relevant work experience is also helpful.

EXPLORING

You can get general business experience by taking on clerical or book-keeping responsibilities with a school club or other organization. Volunteering in your school office is an ideal introduction to office work. This will allow you to become more familiar with computer programs often used in offices and practice business skills such as opening and sorting mail, answering telephones, and filing documents.

Community colleges and other institutions may offer basic or advanced computer training courses for students of all ages. After high school, you may want to explore work-study programs where you can work part-time and gain on-the-job training with local businesses while earning your degree.

EMPLOYERS

Approximately 1.5 million office administrators are employed in the United States. Administrators are needed in all types of offices that have staffs large enough to warrant a manager. The federal government is a major employer of office administrators. Other job opportunities are found in private companies with large clerical staffs, such as hospitals, banks, and telecommunications companies.

STARTING OUT

To break into this career, you should contact the personnel offices of individual firms directly. This is especially appropriate if you have previous clerical experience. College placement offices or other job placement offices may also know of openings. You can also locate jobs through help wanted advertisements. Another option is to sign up with a temporary employment service. Working as a "temp" provides the advantage of getting a firsthand look at a variety of office settings and making many contacts.

Often, a firm will recruit office administrators from its own clerical staff. A clerk with potential supervisory abilities may be given periodic supervisory responsibilities. Later, when an opening occurs for an administrator, that person may be promoted to a full-time position.

ADVANCEMENT

Skilled administrators may be promoted to group manager positions. Promotions, however, often depend on the individual's level of education and other appropriate training, such as training in the company's computer system. Firms usually encourage their employees to pursue further education and may even pay for some tuition costs. Supervisory and management skills can be obtained through company training or community colleges and local vocational schools.

Some companies will prepare office clerks for advancement to administrative positions by having them work in several company departments. This broad experience allows the administrator to better coordinate numerous activities and make more knowledgeable decisions.

EARNINGS

According to OfficeTeam, an administrative staffing company, office managers earned between $27,500 and $35,000 a year in 2002. Senior office managers earned between $33,500 and $44,000.

The Bureau of Labor Statistics reports that office administrators earned an average of about $38,820 a year in 2002. Fifty percent earned between $29,960 and $50,660 a year. The lowest paid 10 percent earned less than $23,630, and the top 10 percent earned over $65,180.

The size and geographic location of the company and the person's individual skills can be key determinants of earnings. Higher wages will be paid to those who work for larger private companies located in and around major metropolitan areas. Full-time workers also receive paid vacations and health and life insurance. Some companies offer year-end bonuses and stock options.

WORK ENVIRONMENT

As is the case with most office workers, office administrators work an average of 35–40 hours a week, although overtime is not unusual. Depending on the company, night, weekend, holiday, or shift work may be expected. Most offices are pleasant places to work. The environment is usually well ventilated and well lighted, and the work is not physically strenuous. The administrator's job can be stressful, however, as it entails supervising a variety of employees with different personalities, temperaments, and work habits.

OUTLOOK

According to the U.S. Department of Labor, the employment rate for office administrators is projected to change little or grow at a rate more slowly than the average for all occupations through 2012. The increased use of data processing and other automated equipment as well as corporate downsizing may reduce the number of administrators in the next decade. However, this profession will still offer good employment prospects because of its sheer size. A large number of job openings will occur as administrators transfer to other industries or leave the workforce for other reasons. Since some clerical occupations will be affected by increased automation, some office administrators may have smaller staffs and be asked to perform more professional tasks.

The federal government should continue to be a good source for job opportunities. Private companies, particularly those with large clerical staffs, such as hospitals, banks, and telecommunications companies, should also have numerous openings. Employment opportunities will be especially good for those trained to operate computers and other types of modern office machinery.

FOR MORE INFORMATION

For information on seminars, conferences, and news on the industry, contact

American Management Association International
1601 Broadway
New York, NY 10019
Tel: 212-586-8100
Email: custserv@amanet.org
http://www.amanet.org

National Association of Executive Secretaries and
  Administrative Assistants
900 South Washington Street, Suite G-13
Falls Church, VA 22046
Tel: 703-237-8616
http://www.naesaa.com

For a career brochure, contact
National Management Association
2210 Arbor Boulevard
Dayton, OH 45439-1580
Tel: 937-294-0421
Email: nma@nma1.org
http://www.nma1.org

For information on careers and related education, contact
Canadian Management Centre of AMA International
150 York Street, 5th Floor
Toronto, ON M5H 3S5 Canada
Tel: 800-262-9699
Email: cmcinfo@cmctraining.org
http://www.cmcamai.org

Office Clerks

QUICK FACTS

School Subjects
Business
English
Mathematics

Personal Skills
Communication/ideas
Following instructions

Work Environment
Primarily indoors
Primarily one location

Minimum Education Level
High school diploma

Salary Range
$14,260 to $22,280 to
$34,890+

Certification or Licensing
None available

Outlook
About as fast as the average

DOT
209

GOE
07.07.03

NOC
1411

O*NET-SOC
43-9061.00

OVERVIEW

Office clerks perform a variety of clerical tasks that help an office run smoothly, including file maintenance, mail sorting, and recordkeeping. In large companies, office clerks might have specialized tasks such as inputting data into a computer, but in most cases, clerks are flexible and have many duties including typing, answering telephones, taking messages, making photocopies, and preparing mailings. Office clerks usually work under close supervision, often with experienced clerks directing their activities. There are approximately 3 million office clerks employed in the United States.

HISTORY

Before the 18th century, many businesspeople did their own office work, such as shipping products, accepting payments, and recording inventory. The industrial revolution changed the nature of business by popularizing the specialization of labor, which allowed companies to increase their output dramatically. At this time, office clerks were brought in to handle the growing amount of clerical duties.

Office workers have become more important as computers, word processors, and other technological advances have increased both the volume of business information available and the speed with which administrative decisions can be made. The number of office workers in the United States has grown as more trained personnel are needed to handle the volume of business communication and information. Businesses and government agencies depend on skilled office workers to file and sort documents, operate office equipment, and cooperate with others to ensure the flow of information.

THE JOB

Office clerks usually perform a variety of tasks as part of their overall job responsibility. They may type or file bills, statements, and business correspondence. They may stuff envelopes, answer telephones, and sort mail. Office clerks also enter data into computers, run errands, and operate office equipment such as photocopiers, fax machines, and switchboards. In the course of an average day, an office clerk usually performs a combination of these and other clerical tasks, spending an hour or so on one task and then moving on to another as directed by an office manager or other supervisor.

An office clerk may work with other office personnel, such as a bookkeeper or accountant, to maintain a company's financial records. The clerk may type and mail invoices and sort payments as they come in, keep payroll records, or take inventories. With more experience, the clerk may be asked to update customer files to reflect receipt of payments and verify records for accuracy.

Office clerks often deliver messages from one office worker to another, an especially important responsibility in larger companies. Clerks may relay questions and answers from one department head to another. Similarly, clerks may relay messages from people outside the company or employees who are outside of the office to those working in house. Office clerks may also work with other personnel on individual projects, such as preparing a yearly budget or making sure a mass mailing gets out on time.

Administrative clerks assist in the efficient operation of an office by compiling business records; providing information to sales personnel and customers; and preparing and sending out bills, policies, invoices, and other business correspondence. Administrative clerks may also keep financial records and prepare the payroll. *File clerks* review and classify letters, documents, articles, and other information and then file this material so it can be quickly retrieved at a later time. They contribute to the smooth distribution of information at a company.

Some clerks have titles that describe where they work and the jobs they do. For example, *congressional-district aides* work for the elected officials of their U.S. congressional district. *Police clerks* handle routine office procedures in police stations, and *concrete products dispatchers* work with construction firms on building projects.

REQUIREMENTS

High School

To prepare for a career as an office clerk, you should take courses in English, mathematics, and as many business-related subjects, such as keyboarding and bookkeeping, as possible. Many community colleges and vocational schools offer business education courses that provide training for general office workers.

Postsecondary Training

A high school diploma is usually sufficient for beginning office clerks, although business courses covering office machine operation and bookkeeping are also helpful. To succeed in this field, you should have computer skills, the ability to concentrate for long periods of time on repetitive tasks, good English and communication skills, and mathematical abilities. Legible handwriting is also a necessity.

Other Requirements

To find work as an office clerk, you should have an even temperament, strong communication skills, and the ability to work well with others. You should find systematic and detailed work appealing. Other personal qualifications include dependability, trustworthiness, and a neat personal appearance.

EXPLORING

You can gain experience by taking on clerical or bookkeeping responsibilities with a school club or other organization. In addition, some school work-study programs may provide opportunities for part-time on-the-job training with local businesses. You may also be able to get a part-time or summer job in a business office by contacting businesses directly or enlisting the aid of a guidance counselor. Training in the operation of business machinery (computers, word processors, and so on) may be available through evening courses offered by business schools and community colleges.

EMPLOYERS

Approximately 3 million office clerks are employed throughout the United States. Major employers include local government, utility companies, insurance agencies, and finance, real estate, and other large firms. Smaller companies also hire office workers and sometimes offer a greater opportunity to gain experience in a variety of clerical tasks.

Office clerks must know how to operate all types of office equipment.
(Getty Images)

STARTING OUT

When you are interested in securing an entry-level position, you should
contact businesses or government agencies directly. Newspaper ads

Books to Read

Bailey-Hughes, Brenda. *The Administrative Assistant*. Menlo Park, Calif.: Crisp Publications, 1998.

Burke, Michelle Marie. *The Valuable Office Professional: For Administrative Assistants, Office Managers, Secretaries, and Other Support Staff*. New York: AMACOM, 1996.

Clark, Lyn R., et al. *HOW 10: A Handbook for Office Workers*. 10th ed. Mason, Ohio: South-Western College Publishing, 2003.

Jean, Anna-Carin. *The Organizer: Secrets & Systems from the World's Top Executive Assistants*. New York: HarperCollins, 1998.

Sabin, William A. *The Gregg Reference Manual*. 9th ed. Columbus, Ohio: Glencoe McGraw Hill, 2000.

Wisinski, Jerry. *Building a Partnership with Your Boss: A Take-Charge Assistant Book*. New York: AMACOM, 1999.

and temporary-work agencies are also good sources for finding jobs in this area. Most companies provide on-the-job training, during which company policies and procedures are explained.

ADVANCEMENT

Office clerks usually begin their employment performing more routine tasks such as delivering messages and sorting and filing mail. With experience, they may advance to more complicated assignments and assume a greater responsibility for the entire project to be completed. Those who demonstrate the desire and ability may move to other clerical positions, such as secretary or receptionist. Clerks with good leadership skills may become group managers or supervisors. To be promoted to a professional occupation such as accountant, a college degree or other specialized training is usually necessary.

The high turnover rate that exists among office clerks increases promotional opportunities. The number and kind of opportunities, however, usually depend on the place of employment and the ability, education, and experience of the employee.

EARNINGS

Salaries for office clerks vary depending on the size and geographic location of the company and the skills of the worker. According to the U.S. Department of Labor, the median salary for full-time office clerks was $22,280 in 2002. The lowest paid 10 percent earned less than $14,260, while the highest paid group earned more than $34,890. Some of the highest paid office clerks worked in local government, while some of the lowest paid worked for employment service firms.

Full-time workers generally receive paid vacations, health insurance, sick leave, and other benefits.

WORK ENVIRONMENT

As is the case with most office workers, office clerks work an average 37–40-hour week. They usually work in comfortable surroundings and are provided with modern equipment. Although clerks have a variety of tasks and responsibilities, the job itself can be fairly routine and repetitive. Clerks often interact with accountants and other office personnel and may work under close supervision.

OUTLOOK

Although employment of clerks is expected to grow only about as fast as the average through 2012, there will still be many jobs available due to the vastness of this field and a high turnover rate. With the increased use of data processing equipment and other types of automated office machinery, more and more employers are hiring people proficient in a variety of office tasks.

Because they are so versatile, office workers can find employment in virtually any kind of industry. In general, companies hire more general office workers when the economy is doing well. In addition to private companies, the federal government should continue to be a good source of jobs. Employment opportunities should be especially good for those trained in various computer skills as well as other office machinery. Temporary and part-time work opportunities should also increase, especially during busy business periods.

FOR MORE INFORMATION

For information on seminars, conferences, and news on the industry, contact

National Association of Executive Secretaries and
    Administrative Assistants
900 South Washington Street, Suite G-13
Falls Church, VA 22046
Tel: 703-237-8616
http://www.naesaa.com

For free office career and salary information, visit the following website:

OfficeTeam
http://www.officeteam.com

Personnel and Labor Relations Specialists

OVERVIEW

Personnel specialists, also known as *human resources professionals,* formulate policy and organize and conduct programs relating to all phases of personnel activity. *Labor relations specialists* serve as mediators between employees and the employer. They represent management during the collective-bargaining process when contracts with employees are negotiated. They also represent the company at grievance hearings, required when a worker feels management has not fulfilled its end of an employment contract. There are approximately 677,000 personnel specialists employed in the United States.

HISTORY

The concept of personnel work developed as businesses grew in size from small owner-operated affairs to large corporate structures with many employees. As these small businesses became larger, it became increasingly difficult for owners and managers to stay connected and in touch with all their employees and still run the day-to-day operations of the business. Smart business owners and managers, however, were aware that the success of their companies depended upon attracting good employees, matching them to jobs they were suited for, and motivating them to do their best. To meet these needs, the personnel department was established, headed by a specialist or staff of specialists whose job was to oversee all aspects of employee relations.

The field of personnel, or human resources, grew as business owners and managers became more aware of the importance of human psychology in managing employees. The development of more sophisticated business methods, the rise of labor unions, and the enactment of government laws and regulations concerned with the welfare and rights of employees have all created an even greater need for personnel specialists who can balance the needs of both employees and employers for the benefit of all.

The development and growth of labor unions in the late 1700s and early 1800s created the need for a particular kind of personnel specialist—one who could work as a liaison between a company's management and its unionized employees. Labor relations specialists often try to arbitrate, or settle, employer-employee disagreements. One of the earliest formal examples of this sort of arbitration in the United States was the first arbitral tribunal created by the New York Chamber of Commerce in 1768. Although arbitration resolutions were often ignored by the courts in preindustrial United States, by the end of World War I, the court system was overwhelmed by litigation—and in 1925 the Federal Arbitration Act was passed, which enforced arbitration agreements reached independent of the courts. Today, personnel and labor relations workers are an integral part of the corporate structure to promote and communicate the needs of workers to management.

THE JOB

Personnel and labor relations specialists are the liaisons between the management of an organization and its employees. They see that management makes effective use of employees' skills, while at the same time improving working conditions for employees and helping them find fulfillment in their jobs. Most positions in this field involve heavy contact with people, at both management and nonmanagement levels.

Both personnel specialists and labor relations specialists are experts in employer-employee relations, although the labor relations specialists concentrate on matters pertaining to union members. Personnel specialists interview job applicants and select or recommend those who seem best suited to the company's needs. Their choices for hiring and advancement must follow federal guidelines for equal employment opportunity and affirmative action. Personnel specialists also plan and maintain programs for wages and salaries, employee benefits, and training and career development.

In small companies, one person often handles all the personnel work. This is the case for Susan Eckerle, human resources manager for Crane Federal Credit Union. She is responsible for all aspects of personnel management for 50 employees who work at three different locations. "I handle all hiring, employee relations counseling, corrective action, administration of benefits, and termination," she says. When Eckerle started working for the credit union, there was no specific human resources department. Therefore, much of her time is spent establishing policies and procedures to ensure that personnel matters run smoothly and consistently. "I've had to write job descriptions, set up interview procedures, and write the employee handbook," she says. "In addition, we don't have a long-term disability plan, and I think we need one. So I've been researching that."

Although Eckerle handles all phases of the human resources process, this is not always the case. The personnel department of a large organization may be staffed by many specialists, including recruiters, interviewers, job analysts, and specialists in charge of benefits, training, and labor relations. In addition, a large personnel department might include *personnel clerks* and assistants who issue forms, maintain files, compile statistics, answer inquiries, and do other routine tasks.

Personnel managers and *employment managers* are concerned with the overall functioning of the personnel department and may be involved with hiring, employee orientation, record keeping, insurance reports, wage surveys, budgets, grievances, and analyzing statistical data and reports. *Industrial relations directors* formulate the policies to be carried out by the various department managers.

Of all the personnel specialists, the one who first meets new employees is often the recruiter. Companies depend on *personnel recruiters* to find the best employees available. To do this, recruiters develop sources through contacts within the community. In some cases, they travel extensively to other cities or to college campuses to meet with college placement directors, attend campus job fairs, and conduct preliminary interviews with potential candidates.

Employment interviewers interview applicants to fill job vacancies, evaluate their qualifications, and recommend hiring the most promising candidates. They sometimes administer tests, check references and backgrounds, and arrange for indoctrination and training. They must also be familiar and current with guidelines for equal employment opportunity (EEO) and affirmative action.

In very large organizations, the complex and sensitive area of EEO is handled by specialists who may be called *EEO representatives,* *affirmative-action coordinators,* or *job development specialists.* These specialists develop employment opportunities and on-the-job training programs for minority or disadvantaged applicants; devise systems or set up representative committees through which grievances can be investigated and resolved as they come up; and monitor corporate practices to prevent possible EEO violations. Preparing and submitting EEO statistical reports is also an important part of their work.

Job analysts are sometimes also called *compensation analysts.* They study all of the jobs within an organization to determine job and worker requirements. Through observation and interviews with employees, they gather and analyze detailed information about job duties and the training and skills required. They write summaries describing each job, its specifications, and the possible route to advancement. Job analysts classify new positions as they are introduced and review existing jobs periodically. These job descriptions, or position classifications, form a structure for hiring, training, evaluating, and promoting employees, as well as for establishing an equitable pay system.

Occupational analysts conduct technical research on job relationships, functions, and content; worker characteristics; and occupational trends. The results of their studies enable business, industry, and government to utilize the general workforce more effectively.

Developing and administering the pay system is the primary responsibility of the *compensation manager.* With the assistance of other specialists on the staff, compensation managers establish a wage scale designed to attract, retain, and motivate employees. A realistic and fair compensation program takes into consideration company policies, government regulations concerning minimum wages and overtime pay, rates currently being paid by similar firms and industries, and agreements with labor unions. The compensation manager is familiar with all these factors and uses them to determine the compensation package.

Training specialists prepare and conduct a wide variety of education and training activities for both new and existing employees. Training specialists may work under the direction of an *education and training manager.* Training programs may cover such special areas as apprenticeship programs, sales techniques, health and safety practices, and retraining displaced workers. The methods chosen by training specialists for maximum effectiveness may include individual training, group instruction, lectures, demonstrations, meetings, or workshops. Training specialists use such teaching aids as handbooks, demonstration models, multimedia programs, and reference works. These specialists also confer with management and supervisors to determine the needs for new training programs or revision of existing ones, maintain records of all training activities, and evaluate the success of the various programs and methods. Training instructors may work under the direction of an education and training manager. *Coordinators of auxiliary personnel* specialize in training non-professional nursing personnel in medical facilities.

Training specialists may help individuals establish career development goals and set up a timetable in which to strengthen job-related skills and learn new ones. Sometimes this involves outside study paid for by the company or rotation to jobs in different departments of the organization. The extent of the training program and the responsibilities of the training specialists vary considerably, depending on the size of the firm and its organizational objectives.

Benefits managers or *employee-welfare managers* handle benefits programs for employees. The major part of such programs generally involves insurance and pension plans. Since the enactment of the Employee Retirement Income Security Act (ERISA), reporting requirements have become a primary responsibility for personnel departments in large companies. The retirement program for state and local government employees is handled by *retirement officers*. In addition to regular health insurance and pension coverage, employee benefit packages have often grown to include such things as dental insurance, accidental death and disability insurance, automobile insurance, homeowner's insurance, profit sharing and thrift/savings plans, and stock options. The expertise of benefits analysts and administrators is extremely important in designing and carrying out the complex programs. These specialists also develop and coordinate additional services related to employee welfare, such as car pools, child care, cafeterias and lunchrooms, newsletters, annual physical exams, recreation and physical fitness programs, and counseling. Personal and financial counseling for employees close to retirement age is growing especially important.

In some cases—especially in smaller companies—the personnel department is responsible for administering the occupational safety and health programs. The trend, however, is toward establishing a separate safety department under the direction of a safety engineer, industrial hygienist, or other safety and health professionals.

Personnel departments may have access to resources outside the organization. For example, *employer relations representatives* promote the use of public employment services and programs among local employers. *Employee-health maintenance program specialists* help set up local government-funded programs among area employers to provide assistance in treating employees with alcoholism or behavioral medical problems.

In companies where employees are covered by union contracts, labor relations specialists form the link between union and management. Prior to negotiation of a collective-bargaining agreement, *labor relations managers* counsel management on their negotiating position and provide background information on the provisions of the current contract and the significance of the proposed changes. They also provide reference materials and statistics pertaining to labor legislation, labor market conditions, prevailing union and management practices, wage and salary surveys, and employee benefit programs. This work requires that labor relations managers be familiar with sources of economic and wage data and have an extensive knowledge of labor law and collective-bargaining trends. In the actual negotiation, the employer is usually represented by the director of labor relations or another top-level official, but the members of the company's labor relations staff play an important role throughout the negotiations.

Specialists in labor relations, or union-management relations, usually work for unionized organizations, helping company officials prepare for collective-bargaining sessions, participating in contract negotiations, and handling day-to-day labor relations matters. A large part of the work of labor relations specialists is analyzing and interpreting the contract for management and monitoring company practices to ensure their adherence to the terms. Of particular importance is the handling of grievance procedures. To investigate and settle grievances, these specialists arrange meetings between workers who raise a complaint, managers and supervisors, and a union representative. A grievance, for example, may concern seniority rights during a layoff. Labor relations disputes are sometimes investigated and resolved by *professional conciliators* or *mediators*. Labor relations work requires keeping up-to-date on developments in labor law, including arbitration decisions, and maintaining close contact with union officials.

Government personnel specialists do essentially the same work as their counterparts in business, except that they deal with public employees whose jobs are subject to civil service regulations. Much government personnel work concentrates on job analysis, because civil service jobs are strictly classified as to entry requirements, duties, and wages. In response to the growing importance of training and career development in the public sector, however, an entire industry of educational and training consultants has sprung up to provide similar services for public agencies. The increased union strength among government workers has resulted in a need for more highly trained labor relations specialists to handle negotiations, grievances, and arbitration cases on behalf of federal, state, and local agencies.

REQUIREMENTS

High School

To prepare for a career as a personnel or labor relations specialist, you should take high school classes that will help prepare you for college. A solid background in the basics—math, science, and English—should be helpful in college-level work. Focus on classes that will help you understand and communicate easily with people. Psychology, English, and speech classes are all good choices. Business classes can help you understand the fundamental workings of the business world, which is also important. Finally, foreign language skills could prove very helpful, especially in areas where there are large numbers of people who speak a language other than English.

Postsecondary Training

High school graduates may start out as personnel clerks and advance to a professional position through experience, but such situations are becoming rare. Most employers require personnel specialists and labor relations specialists to have a college degree. After high school, Susan Eckerle attended a four-year college and received a bachelor's degree in retail management, with a minor in psychology. She says that if she were starting over now, however, she would get a degree in human resources instead.

There is little agreement as to what type of undergraduate training is preferable for personnel and labor relations work. Some employers favor college graduates who have majored in personnel administration or industrial and labor relations, while others prefer individuals with a general business background. Another opinion is to have a well-rounded liberal arts education, with a degree in psychology, sociology, counseling, or education. A master's degree in business administration is also considered suitable preparation. Students interested in personnel might benefit from a degree in personnel administration, political science, or public administration.

Individuals preparing for a career as a personnel specialist will benefit from a wide range of courses. Classes might include business administration, public administration, psychology, sociology, political science, and statistics. For prospective labor relations specialists, valuable courses include labor law, collective bargaining, labor economics, labor history, and industrial psychology.

Work in labor relations may require graduate study in industrial or labor relations. While not required for entry-level jobs, a law degree is extremely useful for contract negotiators and mediators. A combination of industrial relations courses and a law degree is even more desirable. For a career as a professional arbitrator, a degree in industrial and labor relations, law, or personnel management is required.

Certification or Licensing

Some organizations for human resources professionals offer certification programs, which usually consist of a series of classes and a test. For example, the International Foundation of Employee Benefits Plans offers the certified employee benefits specialist designation to candidates who complete a series of college-level courses and pass exams on employee benefits plans. The Society for Human Resources Management has two levels of certification, both of which require experience and a passing score on an exam. Though voluntary, certification is highly recommended and can improve chances for advancement.

Other Requirements

Personnel and labor relations specialists must be able to communicate effectively and clearly both in speech and in writing and deal comfortably and easily with people of different levels of education and experience. "You've got to be people oriented," says Eckerle. "You have to love people and like working with them. That is huge."

Objectivity and fair-mindedness are also necessary in this job, where you often need to consider matters from both the employee's and the employer's point of view. "Being the liaison between management and employees can put you in a tough spot sometimes," Eckerle says. "You're directly between the two poles, and you have to be able to work with both sides."

These workers cooperate as part of a team; at the same time, they must be able to handle responsibility individually. Eckerle says it is important to be organized because you are often responsible for tracking many different things regarding many different people. "You can't be sloppy in your work habits, because you're dealing with a lot of important information and it all has to be processed correctly," she says.

EXPLORING

If you enjoy working with others, you can find helpful experience in managing school teams, planning banquets or picnics, working in your dean's or counselor's office, or reading books about personnel practices in businesses. You might also contact and interview the personnel director of a local business to find out more about the day-to-day responsibilities of this job. Part-time and summer employment in firms that have a personnel department are very good ways to explore the personnel field. Large department stores usually have personnel departments and should not be overlooked as a source of temporary work.

EMPLOYERS

Personnel specialists work in virtually every industry. The majority of the approximately 677,000 personnel specialists working today are employed in the private sector. The biggest employers are professional, scientific, and technical services, manufacturing companies, health care, finance and insurance firms, and administrative and support services. Government is the other large employer of personnel specialists. The companies that are most likely to hire personnel specialists are the larger ones, which have more employees to manage.

STARTING OUT

Colleges and universities have placement counselors who can help graduates find employment. Also, large companies often send recruiters to campuses looking for promising job applicants. Otherwise, interested individuals may apply directly to local companies.

While still in high school, you may apply for entry-level jobs as a personnel clerk or assistant. Private employment agencies and local offices of the state employment service are other possible sources for work. In addition, newspaper want ads often contain listings of many personnel jobs.

Beginners in personnel work are trained on the job or in formal training programs, where they learn how to classify jobs, interview applicants, or administer employee benefits. Then they are assigned to specialized areas in the personnel department. Some people enter the labor relations field after first gaining experience in general personnel work, but it is becoming more common for qualified individuals to enter that field directly.

ADVANCEMENT

After trainees have mastered basic personnel tasks, they are assigned to specific areas in the department to gain specialized experience. In time, they may advance to supervisory positions or to manager of a major part of the personnel program, such as training, compensation, or EEO/affirmative action. Advancement may also be achieved by moving into a higher position in a smaller organization. A few experienced employees with exceptional ability ultimately become top executives with titles such as director of personnel or director of labor relations. As in most fields, employees with advanced education and a proven track record are the most likely to advance in human resources positions.

EARNINGS

Jobs for personnel and labor relations specialists pay salaries that vary widely depending on the nature of the business and the size and location of the firm, as well as on the individual's qualifications and experience.

According to a survey conducted by the National Association of Colleges and Employers, an entry-level human resources specialist with a bachelor's degree earned $35,400 annually in 2003.

The *Occupational Outlook Handbook* (*OOH*) reports that median annual earnings of human resources managers were $64,710 in 2002. Salaries ranged from less than $36,280 to more than $114,300. The average salary for personnel managers in the federal government was $66,886 in 2002. The *OOH* also reports 2002 median annual earnings for the following workers by specialty: training specialists, $42,800; compensation, benefits, and job analysis specialists, $45,100; and personnel recruiters, $39,410.

WORK ENVIRONMENT

Personnel employees work under pleasant conditions in modern offices. Personnel specialists are seldom required to work more than 35–40 hours per week, although they may do so if they are developing a program or special project. The specific hours you work as a personnel specialist may depend upon which company you work for. "I work Monday through Friday," says Susan Eckerle, "but if you work for a company that has weekend hours, you'll probably have to work some weekends too. If you never work weekends, you won't know your employees."

Labor relations specialists often work longer hours, especially when contract agreements are being prepared and negotiated. The difficult aspects of the work may involve firing people, taking disciplinary actions, or handling employee disputes.

OUTLOOK

Due to the abundance of qualified college graduates entering the workforce, the U.S. Department of Labor predicts that there will be faster than average growth through 2012 for personnel, training, and labor relations specialists. Competition for personnel jobs will continue to be strong. Opportunities will be best in the private sector as businesses continue to increase their staffs as they begin to devote more resources to increasing employee productivity, retraining, safety, and benefits. Employment should also be strong with consulting firms who offer personnel services to business that cannot afford to have their own extensive staffs. As jobs change with new technology, more employers will need training specialists to teach new skills. Personnel specialist jobs may be affected by the trend in corporate downsizing and restructuring.

FOR MORE INFORMATION

For information on standards and procedures in arbitration, contact
American Arbitration Association
335 Madison Avenue
10th Floor
New York, NY 10017
Tel: 800-778-7879
http://www.adr.org

For news and information on compensation and benefits administration, contact
WorldatWork
14040 North Northsight Boulevard
Scottsdale, AZ 85260
Tel: 877-951-9191
http://www.worldatwork.org

For information about the Certified Employee Benefit Specialist Program, contact
International Foundation of Employee
  Benefits Plans
18700 West Bluemound Road
PO Box 69
Brookfield, WI 53008
Tel: 262-786-8670
http://www.ifebp.org

For a list of U.S. and Canadian schools offering degrees in industrial relations and human resource degree programs, contact
Industrial Relations Research Association
121 Labor and Industrial Relations
University of Illinois
504 East Armory, MC-504
Champaign, IL 61820
Email: irra@uiuc.edu
http://www.irra.uiuc.edu

For information on training, job opportunities, human resources publications, or online discussions, contact
International Personnel Management Association for Human Resources
1617 Duke Street
Alexandria, VA 22314
Tel: 703-549-7100
http://www.ipma-hr.org

The Society for Human Resource Management is a great resource for career news and developments in the field.
Society for Human Resource Management
1800 Duke Street
Alexandria, VA 22314
Tel: (800) 283-7476
http://www.shrm.org

INTERVIEW

Renee Jones began her career in human resources (HR) as a human resources assistant for a major book publisher. She is currently a generalist in the human resources department at EmCare Inc., the nation's leading provider of emergency care, located in Dallas, Texas. Renee spoke to the editors of Careers in Focus: Business *about her career.*

Q. What are your main responsibilities on the job?
A. My primary responsibilities are staffing, employee relations, policies, programs, and compensation and benefits. A large part of my job revolves around staffing, which means I'm involved in recruitment and hiring, as well as the employee exit process. Another major part of my job is managing employee relations, or how employees are performing in their jobs and working with

supervisors to help their staff be successful. I am also involved in policies and programs—educating employees on company policy and making sure that policies are being followed. In regard to programs, I plan activities and work with departments to develop a positive work culture. In compensation and benefits I am responsible for monitoring what and how people are paid, as well as the benefits they receive.

Q. How did you first become involved with the human resources field?

A. I started my career as a junior-high English teacher, but decided that I wanted to pursue a career in a business setting. I have family members who are in human resources, and their descriptions of their jobs interested me. When I began looking for my first job in human resources I targeted entry-level positions in companies that would allow me to learn about the field while on the job.

Q. What type of training and education did you pursue to work in this field? Did you complete any internships to prepare for your career?

A. I was completely new to HR when I applied for my first job. Most companies seek HR candidates with degrees in human resources. I have a bachelor's degree in English and a secondary education certification, so when I began looking for my first job in HR, I targeted entry-level positions in industries that were appealing to me based on my background. I landed my first job in children's publishing, which was a good match for me. I began to pick up more specific HR knowledge from various seminars and training classes through my employer. After I had been in the field for almost four years, I pursued and obtained a professional certification in the HR field.

Q. What would you say are the pros and cons of your job?

A. The greatest pro for me is being able to have a positive impact on people in their workplace. It's very gratifying to hear people say that they love their jobs and the company and to know that I play some role in their work experience and environment. People spend more time at work than with friends and family. Helping to make that experience to be as positive as possible is the best part of HR for me.

Two cons come to mind. First, human resources falls into a rare category of being both an internal customer-service and a policy-enforcement department; balancing these two different responsibilities can be tricky. The second, and the most difficult, con for me is the unfortunate but necessary reality of sometimes having to fire people.

Q. What would you say are the most important skills and personal qualities for someone in your field?

A. Very strong communication skills, both verbal and written, are essential. You must pay close attention to detail, because frequently you deal with salary information, and that always has to be right. You also have to love people. Human resources is all about interaction—being on the phone, in meetings, talking to people one on one. You also have to have a positive attitude.

Q. How would someone starting out go about finding work in this field?

A. I would advise keeping up with the Society for Human Resource Management (SHRM) website. Employers post jobs there, but there is also lots of valuable information about the field. Check into local chapters of SHRM and try to attend networking events if you can. The best way in is to network!

Q. What advice would you give to someone who is interested in pursuing an HR career?

A. Interview someone in the field and get a clear picture of what they do. Explore the idea of working in a human resources office, or do an internship so that you can see firsthand how the field works. All of this will give you good working knowledge of human resources, as well as experience to add to your resume.

Public Relations Specialists

OVERVIEW

Public relations (PR) specialists, also referred to as *communications specialists* or *media specialists,* develop and maintain programs that present a favorable public image for an individual or organization. They provide information to the target audience (generally, the public at large) about the client, its goals and accomplishments, and any further plans or projects that may be of public interest.

PR specialists may be employed by corporations, government agencies, nonprofit organizations—almost any type of organization. Many PR specialists hold positions in public relations consulting firms or work for advertising agencies. There are approximately 158,000 public relations specialists in the United States.

HISTORY

The first public relations counsel was a reporter named Ivy Ledbetter Lee, who in 1906 was named press representative for coal-mine operators. Labor disputes were becoming a large concern of the operators, and they had run into problems because of their continual refusal to talk to the press and the hired miners. Lee convinced the mine operators to start responding to press questions and supply the press with information on the mine activities.

During and after World War II, the rapid advancement of communications techniques prompted firms to realize they needed professional help to ensure their messages were given proper public

QUICK FACTS

School Subjects
Business
English
Journalism

Personal Skills
Communication/ideas
Leadership/management

Work Environment
Primarily indoors
One location with some
travel

Minimum Education Level
Bachelor's degree

Salary Range
$24,240 to $41,710 to
$75,100+

Certification or Licensing
Voluntary

Outlook
Much faster than the average

DOT
165

GOE
11.09.03

NOC
5124

O*NET-SOC
11-2031.00, 27-3031.00

attention. Manufacturing firms that had turned their production facilities over to the war effort returned to the manufacture of peacetime products and enlisted the aid of public relations professionals to forcefully bring products and the company name before the buying public.

Large business firms, labor unions, and service organizations, such as the American Red Cross, Boy Scouts of America, and the YMCA, began to recognize the value of establishing positive, healthy relationships with the public that they served and depended on for support. The need for effective public relations was often emphasized when circumstances beyond a company's or institution's control created unfavorable reaction from the public.

Public relations specialists must be experts at representing their clients before the media. The rapid growth of the public relations field since 1945 is testimony to the increased awareness in the professional world of the value of media and the proper public relations approach to an organization's many publics.

THE JOB

Public relations specialists are employed to do a variety of tasks, but their main function is to better the communication and understanding between an organization and its many publics: customers, employees, stockholders, contributors, and competitors. They may be employed primarily as writers, creating reports, news releases, and booklet texts. Others write speeches or create copy for radio, TV, or film sequences. These workers often spend much of their time contacting the press, radio, and TV as well as magazines on behalf of the employer. Some PR specialists work more as editors than writers, fact-checking and rewriting employee publications, newsletters, shareholder reports, and other management communications.

Specialists may choose to concentrate in graphic design, using their background knowledge of art and layout for developing brochures, booklets, and photographic communications. Other PR workers handle special events, such as press parties, convention exhibits, open houses, or anniversary celebrations.

PR specialists must be alert to any and all company or institutional events that are newsworthy. They prepare news releases and direct them toward the proper media. Specialists working for manufacturers and retailers are concerned with efforts that will promote sales and create goodwill for the firm's products. They work closely with the marketing and sales departments in announcing new products, preparing displays, and attending occasional dealers' conventions.

A large firm may have a *director of public relations* who is a vice president of the company and in charge of a staff that includes writers, artists, researchers, and other specialists. Publicity for an individual or a small organization may involve many of the same areas of expertise but may be carried out by a few people or possibly even one person.

Many PR workers act as consultants (rather than staff) of a corporation, association, college, hospital, or other institution. These workers have the advantage of being able to operate independently, state opinions objectively, and work with more than one type of business or association.

PR specialists are called upon to work with the public opinion aspects of almost every corporate or institutional problem. These can range from the opening of a new manufacturing plant to a college's dormitory dedication to a merger or sale of a company.

Public relations professionals may specialize. *Lobbyists* try to persuade legislators and other office holders to pass laws favoring the interests of the firms or people they represent. *Fund-raising directors* develop and direct programs designed to raise funds for social welfare agencies and other nonprofit organizations.

Early in their careers, public relations specialists become accustomed to having others receive credit for their behind-the-scenes work. The speeches they draft will be delivered by company officers, the magazine articles they prepare may be credited to the president of the company, and they may be consulted to prepare the message to stockholders from the chairman of the board that appears in the annual report.

REQUIREMENTS

High School
While in high school, take courses in English, journalism, public speaking, humanities, and languages because public relations is based on effective communication with others. Courses such as these will develop your skills in written and oral communication as well as provide a better understanding of different fields and industries to be publicized.

Postsecondary Training
Most people employed in public relations service have a college degree. Major fields of study most beneficial to developing the proper skills are public relations, English, communications, and journalism. Some employers feel that majoring in the area in which the

public relations person will eventually work, such as political science, information technology, or engineering, is the best training. A knowledge of business administration is most helpful as is a native talent for selling. A graduate degree may be required for managerial positions. People with a bachelor's degree in public relations can find staff positions with either an organization or a public relations firm.

More than 200 colleges and about 100 graduate schools offer degree programs or special courses in public relations. In addition, many other colleges offer at least courses in the field. Public relations programs are sometimes administered by the journalism or communication departments of schools. In addition to courses in theory and techniques of public relations, interested individuals may study organization, management and administration, and practical applications and often specialize in areas such as business, government, and nonprofit organizations. Other preparation includes courses in creative writing, psychology, communications, advertising, and journalism. Completing a supervised public relations internship is almost a requirement for obtaining a full-time public relations position.

Certification or Licensing
The Public Relations Society of America and the International Association of Business Communicators accredit public relations workers who have at least five years of experience and pass a comprehensive examination. Such accreditation is a sign of competence in this field and gives you an advantage in a competitive job market, but it is not a requirement for employment.

Other Requirements
Today's public relations specialist must be a businessperson first, both to understand how to perform successfully in business and to comprehend the needs and goals of the organization or client. Additionally, the public relations specialist needs to be a strong writer and speaker, with good interpersonal, leadership, organizational, and creative thinking skills.

EXPLORING
Almost any experience in working with other people will help you to develop strong interpersonal skills, which are crucial in public relations. The possibilities are almost endless. Summer work on a newspaper or trade paper or with a radio or television station may give insight into communications media. Working as a volunteer on a

political campaign can help you to understand the ways in which people can be persuaded. Being selected as a page for the U.S. Congress or a state legislature will help you grasp the fundamentals of government processes. A job in retail will help you to understand some of the principles of product presentation. A teaching job will develop your organization and presentation skills. These are just some of the jobs that will let you explore areas of public relations.

EMPLOYERS

Public relations specialists hold about 158,000 jobs. Workers may be paid employees of the organization they represent or they may be part of a public relations firm that works for organizations on a contract basis. Others are involved in fund-raising or political campaigning. Public relations may be done for a corporation, retail business, service company, utility, association, nonprofit organization, or educational institution.

Most PR firms are located in large cities that are centers of communications. New York, Chicago, Los Angeles, and Washington, D.C., are good places to start a search for a public relations job. However, there is a trend toward public relations firms dispersing across the nation in order to be closer to clients.

STARTING OUT

There is no clear-cut formula for getting a job in public relations. Individuals often enter the field after gaining preliminary experience in another occupation closely allied to the field, usually some segment of communications, and frequently, in journalism. Coming into public relations from newspaper work is still a recommended route. Another good method is to gain initial employment as a public relations trainee or intern, or as a clerk, secretary, or research assistant in a public relations department or a counseling firm.

ADVANCEMENT

In some large companies, an entry-level public relations specialist may start as a trainee in a formal training program for new employees. In others, new employees may expect to be assigned to work that has a minimum of responsibility. They may assemble clippings or do rewrites on material that has already been accepted. They may make posters or assist in conducting polls or surveys, or compile reports from data submitted by others.

As workers acquire experience, they are given more responsibility. They write news releases, direct polls or surveys, or advance to writing speeches for company officials. Progress may seem to be slow, because some skills take a long time to master.

Some advance in responsibility and salary in the same firm in which they started. Others find that the path to advancement is to accept a more attractive position in another firm.

The goal of many public relations specialists is to open an independent office or to join an established consulting firm. To start an independent office requires a large outlay of capital and an established reputation in the field. However, those who are successful in operating their own consulting firms probably attain the greatest financial success in the public relations field.

EARNINGS

The Bureau of Labor Statistics reports that public relations specialists had median annual earnings of $41,710 in 2002. Salaries ranged from less than $24,240 to more than $75,100.

The U.S. Department of Labor reports the following 2002 median salaries for public relations specialists by type of employer: advertising and related services, $48,070; business, professional, labor, and political organizations, $39,330; local government, $42,000; and colleges and universities, $36,820.

Many PR workers receive a range of fringe benefits from corporations and agencies employing them, including bonus/incentive compensation, stock options, profit sharing/pension plans/401(k) programs, medical benefits, life insurance, financial planning, maternity/paternity leave, paid vacations, and family college tuition. Bonuses can range from 5 to 100 percent of base compensation and often are based on individual and/or company performance.

WORK ENVIRONMENT

Public relations specialists generally work in offices with adequate secretarial help, regular salary increases, and expense accounts. They are expected to make a good appearance in tasteful, conservative clothing. They must have social poise, and their conduct in their personal life is important to their firms or their clients. The public relations specialist may have to entertain business associates.

The PR specialist seldom works the conventional office hours for many weeks at a time; although the workweek may consist of 35–40 hours, these hours may be supplemented by evenings and even weekends when meetings must be attended and other special events covered. Time behind the desk may represent only a small part of the total working schedule. Travel is often an important and necessary part of the job.

The life of the PR worker is so greatly determined by the job that many consider this a disadvantage. Because the work is concerned with public opinion, it is often difficult to measure the results of performance and to sell the worth of a public relations program to an employer or client. Competition in the consulting field is keen, and if a firm loses an account, some of its personnel may be affected. The demands it makes for anonymity will be considered by some as one of the profession's less inviting aspects. Public relations involves much more hard work and a great deal less glamour than is popularly supposed.

OUTLOOK

Employment of public relations professionals is expected to grow much faster than the average for all other occupations through 2012, according to the U.S. Department of Labor. Competition will be keen for beginning jobs in public relations because so many job seekers are enticed by the perceived glamour and appeal of the field; those with a bachelor's degree in a communications field and who have completed an internship will have an advantage.

Most large companies have some sort of public relations resource, either through their own staff or through the use of a firm of consultants. They are expected to expand their public relations activities and create many new jobs. More of the smaller companies are hiring public relations specialists, adding to the demand for these workers.

FOR MORE INFORMATION

To read Communication World Online *and other information for professionals in public relations, employee communications, marketing communications, and public affairs, contact*

**International Association of Business
  Communicators**
One Hallidie Plaza, Suite 600
San Francisco, CA 94102
Tel: 415-544-4700
http://www.iabc.com

For statistics, salary surveys, and other information about the profession, contact
Public Relations Society of America
33 Maiden Lane
New York, NY 10038
Tel: 212-460-1490
Email: hq@prsa.org
http://www.prsa.org

This professional association for public relations professionals offers an accreditation program and opportunities for professional development.
Canadian Public Relations Society, Inc.
4195 Dundas Street West, Suite 346
Toronto, ON M8X 1Y4
Canada
Tel: 416-239-7034
http://www.cprs.ca

Purchasing Agents

OVERVIEW

Purchasing agents work for businesses and other large organizations, such as hospitals, universities, and government agencies. They buy raw materials, machinery, supplies, and services required for the organization. They must consider cost, quality, quantity, and time of delivery. Purchasing managers and agents hold approximately 527,000 jobs in the United States.

HISTORY

Careers in the field of purchasing are relatively new and came into real importance only in the last half of the 20th century. The first purchasing jobs emerged during the industrial revolution, when manufacturing plants and businesses became bigger. This led to the division of management jobs into various specialties, one of which was buying.

By the late 1800s, buying was considered a separate job in large businesses. Purchasing jobs were especially important in the railroad, automobile, and steel industries. The trend toward creating specialized buying jobs was reflected in the founding of professional organizations, such as the National Association of Purchasing Agents (now the Institute for Supply Management) and the American Purchasing Society. It was not until after World War II, however, with the expansion of the U.S. government and the increased complexity of business practices, that the job of purchasing agent became firmly established.

THE JOB

Purchasing agents generally work for organizations that buy at least $100,000 worth of goods a year. Their primary goal is to purchase the best quality materials for the best price. To do this, the agent must consider the exact specifications for the required items, cost, quantity discounts, freight handling or other transportation costs, and delivery time. In the past, much of this information was obtained by comparing listings in catalogs and trade journals, interviewing suppliers' representatives, keeping up with current market trends, examining sample goods, and observing demonstrations of equipment. Increasingly, information can be found through computer databases. Sometimes agents visit plants of company suppliers. The agent is responsible for following up on orders and ensuring that goods meet the order specifications.

Most purchasing agents work in firms that have fewer than five employees in the purchasing department. In some small organizations, there is only one person responsible for making purchases. Very large firms, however, may employ as many as 100 purchasing agents, each responsible for specific types of goods. In such organizations there is usually a *purchasing director* or *purchasing manager.*

Some purchasing agents seek the advice of purchase-price analysts, who compile and analyze statistical data about the manufacture and cost of products. Based on this information, they can make recommendations to purchasing personnel regarding the feasibility of producing or buying certain products and suggest ways to reduce costs.

Purchasing agents often specialize in a particular product or field. For example, procurement engineers specialize in aircraft equipment. They establish specifications and requirements for construction, performance, and testing of equipment.

Field contractors negotiate with farmers to grow or purchase fruits, vegetables, or other crops. These agents may advise growers on methods, acreage, and supplies, and arrange for financing, transportation, or labor recruitment.

Head tobacco buyers are engaged in the purchase of tobacco on the auction warehouse floor. They advise other buyers about grades and quantities of tobacco and suggest prices.

Grain buyers manage grain elevators. They are responsible for evaluating and buying grain for resale and milling. They are concerned with the quality, market value, shipping, and storing of grain.

Grain broker-and-market operators buy and sell grain for investors through the commodities exchange. Like other brokers, they work on a commission basis.

REQUIREMENTS

High School

Most purchasing and buying positions require at least a bachelor's degree. Therefore, while in high school, take a college preparatory curriculum. Helpful subjects include English, business, mathematics, social science, and economics.

Postsecondary Training

Although it is possible to obtain an entry-level purchasing job with only a high school diploma, many employers prefer or require college graduates for the job. College work should include courses in general economics, purchasing, accounting, statistics, and business management. Knowledge of computers, especially word processing and spreadsheet programs, is a must. Some colleges and universities offer majors in purchasing, but other business-related majors are appropriate as well.

Purchasing agents with a master's degree in business administration, engineering, technology, or finance tend to have the best jobs and highest salaries. Companies that manufacture machinery or chemicals may require a degree in engineering or a related field. A civil service examination is required for employment in government purchasing positions.

Certification or Licensing

There are no specific licenses or certification requirements imposed by law for purchasing agents. There are, however, several professional organizations to which many purchasing agents belong, including the Institute for Supply Management, the National Institute of Governmental Purchasing, and the American Purchasing Society. These organizations offer certification to applicants who meet their educational and other requirements and who pass the necessary examinations.

The Institute for Supply Management offers the accredited purchasing practitioner (APP) and certified purchasing manager (CPM) designations. The National Institute of Governmental Purchasing offers the certified public purchasing officer (CPPO) and the certified professional public buyer (CPPB) designations. The American Purchasing Society offers the certified purchasing professional (CPP) and certified purchasing manager (CPM) designations. Although certification is not essential, it is a recognized mark of professional competence that enhances a purchasing agent's opportunities for promotion to top management positions.

Books to Read

Antonette, Gerald, Chris Sawchuk, and Larry C. Giunipero. *EPurchasing Plus*. 2d ed. Goshen, N.Y.: JGC Enterprises, 2002.

Banning, Kent. *Opportunities in Purchasing Careers*. New York: McGraw-Hill/Contemporary Books, 1997.

Cavinato, Joseph L. *The Purchasing Handbook: A Guide for the Purchasing and Supply Professional*. 6th ed. New York: McGraw-Hill, 1999.

King, Donald B., and James J. Ritterskamp. *Purchasing Manager's Desk Book of Purchasing Law*. 3rd ed. Upper Saddle River, N.J.: Prentice Hall, 1998.

Neef, Dale. *e-Procurement: From Strategy to Implementation*. Old Tappan, N.J.: Financial Times/Prentice Hall, 2001.

Nelson, Dave, Patricia E. Moody, and Jonathan Stegner. *The Purchasing Machine: How the Top Ten Companies Use Best Practices to Manage Their Supply Chains*. New York: Free Press, 2001.

Poirier, Charles C., and Michael J. Bauer. *E-Supply Chain: Using the Internet to Revolutionize Your Business*. San Francisco, Calif.: Berrett-Koehler Publishing, 2000.

Simchi-Levi, David, Philip Kaminsky, and Edith Simchi-Levy. *Designing and Managing the Supply Chain: Concepts, Strategies, and Cases*. New York: Irwin/McGraw-Hill, 1999.

Other Requirements

Purchasing agents should have calm temperaments and have confidence in their decision-making abilities. Because they work with other people, they need to be diplomatic, tactful, and cooperative. A thorough knowledge of business practices and an understanding of the needs and activities of the employer are essential. It also is helpful to be familiar with social and economic changes in order to predict the amounts or types of products to buy.

EXPLORING

If you are interested in becoming a purchasing agent, you can learn more about the field through a summer job in the purchasing department of a business. Even working as a stock clerk can offer some insight into the job of purchasing agent or buyer. You may also learn about the job by talking with an experienced purchasing agent or reading publications on the field such as *Purchasing* magazine (http://www.manufacturing.net/pur/). Keeping abreast of economic trends, fashion styles, or other indicators may help you to predict the market for particular products. Making educated and informed predictions is a basic part of any buying job.

EMPLOYERS

There are approximately 527,000 purchasing managers and agents (wholesale, retail, farm products, and other) currently working in the United States. They work for a wide variety of businesses, both wholesale and retail, as well as for government agencies. Employers range from small stores, where buying may be only one function of a manager's job, to multinational corporations, where a buyer may specialize in one type of item and buy in enormous quantity. Nearly every business that sells products requires someone to purchase the goods to be sold. These businesses are located nearly everywhere there is a community of people, from small towns to large cities. Of course, the larger the town, the more businesses and thus more buying positions there are. Larger cities provide the best opportunities for higher salaries and advancement.

STARTING OUT

Students without a college degree may be able to enter the field as clerical workers and then receive on-the-job training in purchasing. A college degree, though, is required for most positions. College and university placement services offer assistance to graduating students in locating jobs.

Entry into the purchasing department of a private business can be made by direct application to the company. Some purchasing agents start in another department, such as accounting, shipping, or receiving, and transfer to purchasing when an opportunity arises. Many large companies send newly hired agents through orientation programs, where they learn about goods and services, suppliers, and purchasing methods.

Another means of entering the field is through the military. Service in the Quartermaster Corps of the Army or the procurement divisions of the Navy or Air Force can provide excellent preparation either for a civilian job or a career position in the service.

ADVANCEMENT

In general, purchasing agents begin by becoming familiar with departmental procedures, such as keeping inventory records, filling out forms to initiate new purchases, checking purchase orders, and dealing with vendors. With more experience, they gain responsibility for selecting vendors and purchasing products. Agents may become *junior buyers* of standard catalog items, *assistant buyers,* or managers, perhaps with overall responsibility for purchasing, warehousing, traffic, and related functions. The top positions are *head of purchasing, purchasing director, materials manager,* and *vice-president of purchasing.* These positions include responsibilities concerning production, planning, and marketing.

Many agents advance by changing employers. Frequently an assistant purchasing agent for one firm will be hired as a purchasing agent or head of the purchasing department by another company.

EARNINGS

How much a buyer earns depends on various factors, including the employer's sales volume. Mass merchandisers, such as discount or chain department stores, pay among the highest salaries. According to 2002 data from the U.S. Department of Labor, earnings for purchasing agents ranged from about $27,950 for the lowest 10 percent to more than $73,990 for the top 10 percent. The median salary was $45,090.

Purchasing agents receive the same benefits packages as other employees, such as vacation time, sick leave, life and health insurance, and pension plans.

WORK ENVIRONMENT

Working conditions for a purchasing agent are similar to those of other office employees. They usually work in rooms that are pleasant, well lighted, and clean. Work is year-round and generally steady because it is not particularly influenced by seasonal factors. Most agents have 40-hour workweeks, although overtime is not uncommon. In addition to regular hours, agents may have to attend meetings, read and prepare reports, visit suppliers' plants, or travel. While most work is done indoors, some agents occasionally need to inspect goods outdoors or in warehouses.

It is important for purchasing agents to have good working relations with others. They must interact closely with suppliers as well as with personnel in other departments of the company. Because of the importance of their decisions, purchasing agents sometimes work under great pressure.

OUTLOOK

Although the overall employment growth in the purchasing field is expected to be slower than the average through 2012, employment growth for purchasing agents, except for wholesale and retail, should grow at an average rate. Growth in the purchasing field will be limited by increased use of software and electronic transactions for purchases. But purchasing agents can still find ample opportunities in manufacturing, service, and farm industries, as purchases of complex equipment and testing product quality and freshness (for farm products) cannot be handled electronically.

Demand will be strongest for those with a master's degree in business administration or an undergraduate degree in purchasing. Among firms that manufacture complex machinery, chemicals, and other technical products, the demand will be for graduates with a master's degree in engineering, another field of science, or business administration. Graduates of two-year programs in purchasing or materials management should continue to find good opportunities, especially in smaller companies.

FOR MORE INFORMATION

For career and certification information, contact
American Purchasing Society
North Island Center
8 East Galena Boulevard, Suite 203
Aurora Place, IL 60506
Tel: 630-859-0250
http://www.american-purchasing.com

For career and certification information and lists of colleges with purchasing programs, contact
Institute for Supply
  Management
PO Box 22160
Tempe, AZ 85285
Tel: 800-888-6276
http://www.ism.ws

For an information packet on purchasing careers in government, contact
National Institute of Governmental Purchasing
151 Spring Street
Herndon, VA 20170
Tel: 800-367-6447
http://www.nigp.org

For materials on educational programs in the retail industry, contact
National Retail Federation
325 7th Street, NW, Suite 1100
Washington, DC 20004
Tel: 800-673-4692
http://www.nrf.com

Receptionists

OVERVIEW

Receptionists—so named because they receive visitors in places of business—have the important job of giving a business's clients and visitors a positive first impression. Also called *information clerks,* these front-line workers are the first communication sources who greet clients and visitors to an office, answer their questions, and direct them to the people they wish to see. Receptionists also answer telephones, take and distribute messages for other employees, and make sure no one enters the office unescorted or unauthorized. Many receptionists perform additional clerical duties. *Switchboard operators* perform similar tasks but primarily handle equipment that receives an organization's telephone calls. There are more than 1.1 million receptionists employed throughout the United States.

HISTORY

In the 18th and 19th centuries, as businesses began to compete with each other for customers, merchants and other business people began to recognize the importance of giving customers the immediate impression that the business was friendly, efficient, and trustworthy. These businesses began to employ *hosts* and *hostesses*, workers who would greet customers, make them comfortable, and often serve them refreshments while they waited or did business with the owner. As businesses grew larger and more diverse, these hosts and hostesses (only recently renamed receptionists) took on the additional duties of answering phones, keeping track of workers, and directing visitors to the employee they needed to see. Receptionists also began to work as information dispensers, answering growing numbers of inquiries from the public. In the medical field, as services expanded, more receptionists were needed to direct patients to physicians and clinical services and to keep track of appointments and payment information.

Soon receptionists became indispensable to business and service establishments. Today, it is hard to imagine most medium-sized or large businesses functioning without a receptionist.

THE JOB

The receptionist is a specialist in human contact: The most important part of a receptionist's job is dealing with people in a courteous and effective manner. Receptionists greet customers, clients, patients, and salespeople, take their names, and determine the nature of their business and the person they wish to see. The receptionist then pages the requested person, directs the visitor to that person's office or location, or makes an appointment for a later visit. Receptionists usually keep records of all visits by writing down the visitor's name, purpose of visit, person visited, and date and time.

Most receptionists answer the telephone at their place of employment; many operate switchboards or paging systems. These workers usually take and distribute messages for other employees and may receive and distribute mail. Receptionists may perform a variety of other clerical duties, including keying in and filing correspondence and other paperwork, proofreading, preparing travel vouchers, and preparing outgoing mail. In some businesses, receptionists are responsible for monitoring the attendance of other employees. In businesses where employees are frequently out of the office on assignments, receptionists may keep track of their whereabouts to ensure they receive important phone calls and messages. Many receptionists use computers and word processors in performing their clerical duties.

Receptionists are partially responsible for maintaining office security, especially in large firms. They may require all visitors to sign in and out and carry visitors' passes during their stay. Since visitors may not enter most offices unescorted, receptionists usually accept and sign for packages and other deliveries.

Receptionists are frequently responsible for answering inquiries from the public about a business's nature and operations. To answer these questions efficiently and in a manner that conveys a favorable impression, a receptionist must be as knowledgeable as possible about the business's products, services, policies, and practices and familiar with the names and responsibilities of all other employees. They must be careful, however, not to divulge classified information such as business procedures or employee activities that a competing company might be able to use. This part of a receptionist's job is so important that some businesses call their receptionists information clerks.

A large number of receptionists work in physicians' and dentists' offices, hospitals, clinics, and other health care establishments. Workers in medical offices receive patients, take their names, and escort them to examination rooms. They make future appointments for patients and may prepare statements and collect bill payments. In hospitals, receptionists obtain patient information, assign patients to rooms, and keep records on the dates they are admitted and discharged.

In other types of industries, the duties of these workers vary. Receptionists in hair salons arrange appointments for clients and may escort them to stylists' stations. Workers in bus or train companies answer inquiries about departures, arrivals, and routes. *In-file operators* collect and distribute credit information to clients for credit purposes. *Registrars, park aides,* and *tourist-information assistants* may be employed as receptionists at public or private facilities. Their duties may include keeping a record of the visitors entering and leaving the facility, as well as providing information on services that the facility provides. Information clerks, *automobile club information clerks,* and *referral-and-information aides* provide answers to questions by telephone or in person from both clients and potential clients and keep a record of all inquiries.

Switchboard operators may perform specialized work, such as operating switchboards at police district offices. Or, they may handle airport communication systems, which includes public address paging systems and courtesy telephones, or serve as *answering-service operators,* who record and deliver messages for clients who cannot be reached by telephone.

REQUIREMENTS

High School

You can prepare for a receptionist or switchboard operator position by taking courses in business procedures, office machine operation, business math, English, and public speaking. You should also take computer science courses, as computers are used in nearly all offices.

Postsecondary Training

Most employees require receptionists to have a high school diploma. Some businesses prefer to hire workers who have completed post-high school courses at a junior college or business school. If you are

A receptionist is usually responsible for keeping written records of all office visitors. *(Corbis)*

interested in post-high-school education, you may find courses in basic bookkeeping and principles of accounting helpful. This type of training may lead to a higher paying receptionist job and a better chance for advancement. Many employers require typing, switchboard, computer, and other clerical skills, but they may provide some on-the-job training as the work is typically entry level.

Other Requirements

To be a good receptionist, you must be well groomed, have a pleasant voice, and be able to express yourself clearly. Because you may sometimes deal with demanding people, a smooth, patient disposition and good judgment are important. All receptionists need to be courteous and tactful. A good memory for faces and names also proves very valuable. Most important are good listening and communications skills and an understanding of human nature.

EXPLORING

A good way to obtain experience in working as a receptionist is through a high school work-study program. Students participating in such programs spend part of their school day in classes and the rest working for local businesses. This arrangement will help you gain valuable practical experience before you look for your first job. High school guidance counselors can provide information about work-study opportunities.

EMPLOYERS

According to the U.S. Department of Labor, approximately 1.1 million people are employed as receptionists. Almost 90 percent of these work in service-providing industries. Among service-providing industries, health care and social assistance offices employed almost one- third of receptionists. Factories, wholesale and retail stores, and service providers also employ a large percentage of these workers. Almost one-third of receptionists work part time.

STARTING OUT

While you are in high school, you may be able to learn of openings with local businesses through your school guidance counselors or newspaper want ads. Local state employment offices frequently have information about receptionist work. You should also contact area businesses for whom you would like to work; many available positions are not advertised in the paper because they are filled so quickly. Temporary-work agencies are a valuable resource for finding jobs, too, some of which may lead to permanent employment. Friends and relatives may also know of job openings.

ADVANCEMENT

Advancement opportunities are limited for receptionists, especially in small offices. The more clerical skills and education workers have, the greater their chances for promotion to such better-paying jobs as secretary, administrative assistant, or bookkeeper. College or business school training can help receptionists advance to higher-level positions. Many companies provide training for their receptionists and other employees, helping workers gain skills for job advancement.

EARNINGS

Earnings for receptionists vary widely with the education and experience of the worker and type, size, and geographic location of the business. The median annual salary for receptionists was $21,150 in 2002. According to an OfficeTeam salary survey, receptionists had starting salaries ranging from $19,500 to $25,000 in 2002. In 2003, the U.S. federal government paid starting salaries of $19,898–$23,555 to receptionists with a high school diploma and six months of experience. The median annual salary for receptionists working in the federal government was $25,704 in 2003. Experienced receptionists can make more than $30,130 annually.

Receptionists are usually eligible for paid holidays and vacations, sick leave, medical and life insurance coverage, and a retirement plan of some kind.

WORK ENVIRONMENT

Because receptionists usually work near or at the main entrance to the business, their work area is one of the first places a caller sees. Therefore, these areas are usually pleasant and clean and are carefully furnished and decorated to create a favorable, businesslike impression. Work areas are almost always air-conditioned, well lit, and relatively quiet, although a receptionist's phone rings frequently. Receptionists work behind a desk or counter and spend most of their workday sitting, although some standing and walking is required when filing or escorting visitors to their destinations. The job may be stressful at times, especially when a worker must be polite to rude callers.

Most receptionists work 35–40 hours a week. Some may work weekend and evening hours, especially those in medical offices. Switchboard operators may have to work any shift of the day if their employers require 24-hour phone service, such as hotels and hospitals. These workers usually work holidays and weekend hours.

OUTLOOK

Employment for receptionists is expected to grow faster than the average through 2012, according to the *Occupational Outlook Handbook*. Many openings will occur due to the occupation's high turnover rate. Opportunities will be best for those with wide clerical skills and work experience. Growth in jobs for receptionists is expected to be greater than for other clerical positions because automation will have little effect on the receptionist's largely interpersonal duties and because of an anticipated growth in the number of businesses providing services. In addition, more and more businesses are learning how valuable a receptionist can be in furthering their public relations efforts and helping them convey a positive image. Opportunities should be especially good in rapid services industries, such as physician's offices, law firms, temporary help agencies, and consulting firms.

FOR MORE INFORMATION

For information on careers, contact IAAP.

International Association of Administrative Professionals (IAAP)
10502 NW Ambassador Drive
PO Box 20404
Kansas City, MO 64195
Tel: 816-891-6600
Email: service@iaap-hq.org
http://www.iaap-hq.org

Secretaries

OVERVIEW

Secretaries, also called *administrative assistants*, perform a wide range of jobs that vary greatly from business to business. However, most secretaries key in documents, manage records and information, answer telephones, handle correspondence, schedule appointments, make travel arrangements, and sort mail. The amount of time secretaries spend on these duties depends on the size and type of the office as well as on their own job training. There are approximately 4.1 million secretaries employed in the United States.

HISTORY

Today, as in the past, secretaries play an important role in keeping lines of communication open. Before there were telephones, messages were transmitted by hand, often from the secretary of one party to the secretary of the receiving party. Their trustworthiness was valued because the lives of many people often hung in the balance of certain communications.

Secretaries in the ancient world developed methods of taking abbreviated notes so that they could capture as much as possible of their employers' words. In 16th-century England, the modern precursors of the shorthand methods we know today were developed. In the 19th century, Isaac Pitman and John Robert Gregg developed the shorthand systems that are still used in offices and courtrooms in the United States.

The equipment secretaries use in their work has changed drastically in recent years. Almost every office is automated in some way.

Familiarity with machines such as switchboards, Dictaphones, photocopiers, fax machines, and personal computers has become an integral part of the secretary's day-to-day work.

THE JOB

Secretaries perform a variety of administrative and clerical duties. The goal of all their activities is to assist their employers in the execution of their work and to help their companies conduct business in an efficient and professional manner.

Secretaries' work includes processing and transmitting information to the office staff and to other organizations. They operate office machines and arrange for their repair or servicing. These machines include computers, typewriters, dictating machines, photocopiers, switchboards, and fax machines. These secretaries also order office supplies and perform regular duties such as answering phones, sorting mail, managing files, taking dictation, and composing and keying in letters.

Some offices have word processing centers that handle all of the firm's typing. In such a situation, *administrative secretaries* take care of all secretarial duties except for typing and dictation. This arrangement leaves them free to respond to correspondence, prepare reports, do research and present the results to their employers, and otherwise assist the professional staff. Often these secretaries work in groups of three or four so that they can help each other if one secretary has a workload that is heavier than normal.

In many offices, secretaries make appointments for company executives and keep track of the office schedule. They make travel arrangements for the professional staff or for clients, and occasionally are asked to travel with staff members on business trips. Other secretaries might manage the office while their supervisors are away on vacation or business trips.

Secretaries take minutes at meetings, write up reports, and compose and type letters. They often will find their responsibilities growing as they learn the business. Some are responsible for finding speakers for conferences, planning receptions, and arranging public relations programs. Some write copy for brochures or articles before making the arrangements to have them printed or microfilmed, or they might use desktop publishing software to create the documents themselves. They greet clients and guide them to the proper offices, and they often supervise and train other staff members and newer secretaries, especially in the use of computer software programs.

Some secretaries perform very specialized work. *Legal secretaries* prepare legal papers including wills, mortgages, contracts, deeds, motions, complaints, and summonses. They work under the direct supervision of an attorney or paralegal. They assist with legal research by reviewing legal journals and organizing briefs for their employers. They must learn an entire specialized vocabulary that is used in legal papers and documents.

Medical secretaries take medical histories of patients; make appointments; prepare and send bills to patients; track and collect bills; process insurance billing; maintain medical files; and pursue correspondence with patients, hospitals, and associations. They assist physicians or medical scientists with articles, reports, speeches, and conference proceedings. Some medical secretaries are responsible for ordering medical supplies. They, too, need to learn an entire specialized vocabulary of medical terms and be familiar with laboratory or hospital procedures.

Technical secretaries work for engineers and scientists preparing reports and papers that often include graphics and mathematical equations that are difficult to format on paper. The secretaries maintain a technical library and help with scientific papers by gathering and editing materials.

Social secretaries, often called *personal secretaries*, arrange all of the social activities of their employers. They handle private as well as business social affairs and may plan parties, send out invitations, or write speeches for their employers. Social secretaries are often hired by celebrities or high-level executives who have busy social calendars to maintain.

Many associations, clubs, and nonprofit organizations have *membership secretaries* who compile and send out newsletters or promotional materials while maintaining membership lists, dues records, and directories. Depending on the type of club, the secretary may be the one who gives out information to prospective members and who keeps current members and related organizations informed of upcoming events.

Education secretaries work in elementary or secondary schools or on college campuses. They take care of all clerical duties at the school. Their responsibilities may include preparing bulletins and reports for teachers, parents, or students, keeping track of budgets for school supplies or student activities, and maintaining the school's calendar of events. Depending on the position, they may work for school administrators, principals, or groups of teachers or professors. Other education secretaries work in administration offices, state education departments, or service departments.

Skills for Secretarial Success

The role of the secretary in today's workplace is more diverse than ever before. According to the International Association of Administrative Professionals, the following are just some of the many skills required of today's secretaries:

- project management
- software training
- website maintenance
- negotiation and mediation
- online purchasing
- coordination of mass mailings
- document and information storage and retrieval
- event planning and coordination
- travel planning
- desktop publishing
- PC troubleshooting
- writing, editing, and proofreading

REQUIREMENTS

High School
You will need at least a high school diploma to enter this field. To prepare for a career as a secretary, take high school courses in business, English, and speech. Keyboarding and computer science courses will also be helpful.

Postsecondary Training
To succeed as a secretary, you will need good office skills that include rapid and accurate keyboarding skills and good spelling and grammar. You should enjoy handling details. Some positions require typing a minimum number of words per minute, as well as shorthand ability. Knowledge of word processing, spreadsheet, and database management is important, and most employers require it. Some of these skills can be learned in business education courses taught at vocational and business schools. Special training programs are

available for students who want to become medical or legal secretaries or administrative technology assistants.

Certification or Licensing

Qualifying for the designations certified professional secretary (CPS) or certified administrative professional (CAP) is increasingly recognized in business and industry as a consideration for promotion to a senior level secretary. The International Association of Administrative Professionals gives the examinations required for these certifications. Secretaries with limited experience can become an accredited legal secretary (ALS) by obtaining certification from the Certifying Board of the National Association of Legal Secretaries. Those with at least three years of experience in the legal field can be certified as a professional legal secretary (PLS) from this same organization. Legal Secretaries International offers the certified legal secretary specialist (CLSS) designation in areas such as business law, probate, criminal law, and civil litigation to those who have at least five years of law-related experience and who pass an examination.

Other Requirements

Personal qualities are important in this field of work. As a secretary, you will often be the first employee of a company that clients meet, and therefore you must be friendly, poised, and professionally dressed. Because you must work closely with others, you should be personable and tactful. Discretion, good judgment, organizational ability, and initiative are also important. These traits will not only get you hired but will also help you advance in your career.

Some employers encourage their secretaries to take advanced courses and to be trained to use any new piece of equipment in the office. Requirements vary widely from company to company.

EXPLORING

High school guidance counselors can give interest and aptitude tests to help you assess your suitability for a career as a secretary. Local business schools often welcome visitors, and sometimes offer courses that can be taken in conjunction with a high school business course. Work-study programs will also provide you with an opportunity to work in a business setting to get a sense of the work performed by secretaries.

Part-time or summer jobs as receptionists, file clerks, and office clerks are often available in various offices. These jobs are the best indicators of future satisfaction in the secretarial field. You may find a part-time job if you are computer-literate. Cooperative education programs arranged through schools and "temping" through an agency also are valuable ways to acquire experience. In general, any job that teaches basic office skills is helpful.

EMPLOYERS

There are 4.1 million secretaries employed throughout the United States, making this profession one of the largest in the country. Of this total, 264,000 specialize as legal secretaries and 339,000 work as medical secretaries. Secretaries are employed in almost every type of industry. From health care, banking, financial services, and real estate to construction, manufacturing, transportation, communications, and retail and wholesale trade. A large number of secretaries are employed by federal, state, and local governments.

STARTING OUT

Most people looking for work as secretaries find jobs through the newspaper want ads or by applying directly to local businesses. Both private employment offices and state employment services place secretaries, and business schools help their graduates find suitable jobs. Temporary-help agencies also are an excellent way to find jobs, many of which may turn into permanent ones.

ADVANCEMENT

Secretaries often begin by assisting executive secretaries and work their way up by learning the way their business operates. Initial promotions from a secretarial position are usually to jobs such as secretarial supervisor, office manager, or administrative assistant. Depending on other personal qualifications, college courses in business, accounting, or marketing can help the ambitious secretary enter middle and upper management. Training in computer skills can also lead to advancement. Secretaries who become proficient in word processing, for instance, can get jobs as instructors or as sales representatives for software manufacturers.

Many legal secretaries, with additional training and schooling, become paralegals. Secretaries in the medical field can advance into the fields of radiological and surgical records or medical transcription.

EARNINGS

Salaries for secretaries vary widely by region; type of business; and the skill, experience, and level of responsibility of the secretary. Secretaries (except legal and medical, and executive) earned an average of $25,290 annually in 2002. Medical secretaries earned salaries that ranged from less than $18,310 to $37,550 or more per year in 2002, according to the Department of Labor. Legal secretaries made an average of $35,020 in 2002. Salaries for legal secretaries ranged from $21,990 to more than $54,810 annually. An attorney's rank in the firm will also affect the earnings of a legal secretary; secretaries who work for a partner will earn higher salaries than those who work for an associate.

Secretaries, especially those working in the legal profession, earn considerably more if certified. Most secretaries receive paid holidays and two weeks vacation after a year of work, as well as sick leave. Many offices provide benefits including health and life insurance, pension plans, overtime pay, and tuition reimbursement.

WORK ENVIRONMENT

Most secretaries work in pleasant offices with modern equipment. Office conditions vary widely, however. While some secretaries have their own offices and work for one or two executives, others share crowded workspace with other workers.

Most office workers work 35–40 hours a week. Very few secretaries work on the weekends on a regular basis, although some may be asked to work overtime if a particular project demands it.

The work is not physically strenuous or hazardous, although deadline pressure is a factor and sitting for long periods of time can be uncomfortable. Many hours spent in front of a computer can lead to eyestrain or repetitive-motion problems for secretaries. Most secretaries are not required to travel. Part-time and flexible schedules are easily adaptable to secretarial work.

OUTLOOK

The U.S. Department of Labor predicts that overall employment for secretaries will grow more slowly than the average through 2012. However, opportunities for secretaries who specialize in legal or medical fields will grow about as fast as the average through 2012. Those secretaries who do not specialize in one area can expect slower than average job opportunities. Industries such as administrative and support services, health care and social assistance, private education services, and professional, scientific, and technical services will create the most new job opportunities. As common with large occupations, the need to replace retiring workers will generate many openings.

Computers, fax machines, electronic mail, copy machines, and scanners are some technological advancements that have greatly improved the work productivity of secretaries. Company downsizing and restructuring, in some cases, have redistributed traditional secretarial duties to other employees. There has been a growing trend in assigning one secretary to assist two or more managers, adding to this field's decline. Though more professionals are using personal computers for their correspondence, some administrative duties will still need to be handled by secretaries. The personal aspects of the job and responsibilities such as making travel arrangements, scheduling conferences, and transmitting staff instructions have not changed.

Many employers currently complain of a shortage of capable secretaries. Those with skills (especially computer skills) and experience will have the best chances for employment. Specialized secretaries should attain certification in their field to stay competitive.

FOR MORE INFORMATION

For information on the certified professional secretary designation, contact

International Association of Administrative Professionals
10502 NW Ambassador Drive
PO Box 20404
Kansas City, MO 64195
Tel: 816-891-6600
Email: service@iaap-hq.org
http://www.iaap-hq.org

For information about certification, contact

Legal Secretaries International, Inc.
8902 Sunnywood Drive
Houston, TX 77088
http://www.legalsecretaries.org

For information on the certified professional legal secretary and the accredited legal secretary designations, contact

NALS
314 East 3rd Street, Suite 210
Tulsa, OK 74120
Tel: 918-582-5188
Email: info@nals.org
http://www.nals.org

For information regarding union representation, contact
Office & Professional Employees International Union
265 West 14th Street, Sixth Floor
New York, NY 10011
Tel: 800-346-7348
http://www.opeiu.org

For employment information, contact
OfficeTeam
2884 Sand Hill Road
Menlo Park, CA 94025
Tel: 800-804-8367
http://www.officeteam.com

Stock Clerks

OVERVIEW

Stock clerks receive, unpack, store, distribute, and record the inventory for materials or products used by a company, plant, or store. Approximately 1.6 million stock clerks are employed in the United States.

HISTORY

Almost every type of business establishment imaginable—shoe store, restaurant, hotel, auto repair shop, hospital, supermarket, or steel mill—buys materials or products from outside distributors and uses these materials in its operations. A large part of the company's money is tied up in these inventory stocks, but without them operations would come to a standstill. Stores would run out of merchandise to sell, mechanics would be unable to repair cars until new parts were shipped in, and factories would be unable to operate once their basic supply of raw materials ran out.

To avoid these problems, businesses have developed their own inventory-control systems to store enough goods and raw materials for uninterrupted operations, move these materials to the places they are needed, and know when it is time to order more. These systems are the responsibility of stock clerks.

THE JOB

Stock clerks work in just about every type of industry, and no matter what kind of storage or stock room they staff—food, clothing, merchandise, medicine, or raw materials—the work of stock clerks is essentially the same. They receive, sort, put away, distribute, and keep track of the items a business sells or uses. Their titles sometimes vary based on their responsibilities.

When goods are received in a stockroom, stock clerks unpack the shipment and check the contents against documents such as the invoice, purchase order, and bill of lading, which lists the contents of the shipment. The shipment is inspected, and any damaged goods are set aside. Stock clerks may reject or send back damaged items or call vendors to complain about the condition of the shipment. In large companies, *shipping and receiving clerks* may do this work.

Once the goods are received, stock clerks organize them and sometimes mark them with identifying codes or prices so they can be placed in stock according to the existing inventory system. In this way the materials or goods can be found readily when needed, and inventory control is much easier. In many firms stock clerks use handheld scanners and computers to keep inventory records up to date.

In retail stores and supermarkets, stock clerks may bring merchandise to the sales floor and stock shelves and racks. In stockrooms and warehouses they store materials in bins, on the floor, or on shelves. In other settings, such as restaurants, hotels, and factories, stock clerks deliver goods when they are needed. They may do this on a regular schedule or at the request of other employees or supervisors. Although many stock clerks use mechanical equipment, such as forklifts, to move heavy items, some perform strenuous and laborious work. In general, the work of a stock clerk involves much standing, bending, walking, stretching, lifting, and carrying.

When items are removed from the inventory, stock clerks adjust records to reflect the products' use. These records are kept as current as possible, and inventories are periodically checked against these records. Every item is counted, and the totals are compared with the records on hand or the records from the sales, shipping, production, or purchasing departments. This helps identify how fast items are being used, when items must be ordered from outside suppliers, or even whether items are disappearing from the stockroom. Many retail establishments use computerized cash registers that maintain an inventory count automatically as they record the sale of each item.

The duties of stock clerks vary depending on their place of employment. Stock clerks working in small firms perform many different tasks, including shipping and receiving, inventory control, and purchasing. In large firms, responsibilities may be more narrowly defined. More specific job categories include *inventory clerks, stock control clerks, material clerks, order fillers, merchandise distributors,* and shipping and receiving clerks.

Stock clerks receive, sort, and put away all of the materials a business uses. *(Getty Images)*

At a construction site or factory that uses a variety of raw and finished materials, there are many different types of specialized work for stock clerks. *Tool crib attendants* issue, receive, and store the various hand tools, machine tools, dies, and other equipment used in an industrial establishment. They make sure the tools come back in reasonably good shape and keep track of those that need replacing.

Parts order and stock clerks purchase, store, and distribute the spare parts needed for motor vehicles and other industrial equipment. *Metal control coordinators* oversee the movement of metal stock and supplies used in producing nonferrous metal sheets, bars, tubing, and alloys. In mining and other industries that regularly use explosives, *magazine keepers* store explosive materials and components safely and distribute them to authorized personnel. In the military, *space and storage clerks* keep track of the weights and amounts of ammunition and explosive components stored in the magazines of an arsenal and check their storage condition.

Many types of stock clerks can be found in other industries. At printing companies, *cut-file clerks* collect, store, and hand out the layout cuts, ads, mats, and electrotypes used in the printing process. *Parts clerks* handle and distribute spare and replacement parts in repair and maintenance shops. In eyeglass centers, *prescription clerks* select the lens blanks and frames for making eyeglasses and keep inventory stocked at a specified level. In motion picture companies, *property custodians* receive, store, and distribute the props needed for shooting. In hotels and hospitals, *linen room attendants* issue and keep track of inventories of bed linen, tablecloths, and uniforms, while *kitchen clerks* verify the quantity and quality of food products being taken from the storeroom to the kitchen. Aboard ships, the clerk in charge of receiving and issuing supplies and keeping track of inventory is known as the *storekeeper.*

REQUIREMENTS

High School
Although there are no specific educational requirements for beginning stock clerks, employers prefer to hire high school graduates. Reading and writing skills and a basic knowledge of mathematics are necessary; typing and filing skills are also useful. In the future, as more companies install computerized inventory systems, a knowledge of computer operations will be important.

Other Requirements
Good health and good eyesight is important. A willingness to take orders from supervisors and others is necessary for this work, as is the ability to follow directions. Organizational skills also are important, as is neatness. Depending on where you work, you may be required to join a union. This is especially true of stock clerks who are employed by industry and who work in large cities with a high percentage of union-affiliated companies.

When a stock clerk handles certain types of materials, extra training or certification may be required. Generally those who handle jewelry, liquor, or drugs must be bonded.

EXPLORING

The best way to learn about the responsibilities of a stock clerk is to get a part-time or summer job as a sales clerk, stockroom helper, stockroom clerk, or, in some factories, stock chaser. These jobs are relatively easy to get and can help you learn about stock work, as well as about the duties of workers in related positions. This sort of part-time work can also lead to a full-time job.

EMPLOYERS

About 1.6 million people work as stock clerks. Almost 75 percent of stock clerks work in retail and wholesale firms, and the remainder work in hospitals, factories, government agencies, schools, and other organizations. Nearly all sales-floor stock clerks are employed in retail establishments, especially supermarkets and department stores.

STARTING OUT

Job openings for stock clerks often are listed in newspaper classified ads. Job seekers should contact the personnel office of the firm looking for stock clerks and fill out an application for employment. School counselors, parents, relatives, and friends also can be good sources for job leads and may be able to give personal references if an employer requires them.

Stock clerks usually receive on-the-job training. New workers start with simple tasks, such as counting and marking stock. The basic responsibilities of the job are usually learned within the first few weeks. As they progress, stock clerks learn to keep records of incoming and outgoing materials, take inventories, and place orders. As wholesale and warehousing establishments convert to automated inventory systems, stock clerks need to be trained to use the new equipment. Stock clerks who bring merchandise to the sales floor and stock shelves and sales racks need little training.

ADVANCEMENT

Stock clerks with ability and determination have a good chance of being promoted to jobs with greater responsibility. In small firms, stock clerks may advance to sales positions or become assistant buyers or purchasing agents. In large firms, stock clerks can advance to more responsible stock handling jobs, such as invoice clerk, stock control clerk, and procurement clerk.

Furthering one's education can lead to more opportunities for advancement. By studying at a technical or business school or taking home-study courses, stock clerks can prove to their employer that they have the intelligence and ambition to take on more important tasks. More advanced positions, such as warehouse manager and purchasing agent, are usually given to experienced people who have post-high school education.

EARNINGS

Beginning stock clerks usually earn the minimum wage or slightly more. The U.S. Department of Labor reports that stock clerks earned a median hourly wage of $9.26 in 2002. Based on a 40-hour workweek, this is annual salary of $19,260. Experienced stock clerks can earn anywhere from $23,420 to more than $35,230, with time-and-a-half pay for overtime. Average earnings vary depending on the type of industry and geographic location. Stock clerks working in the retail trade generally earn wages in the middle range. In transportation, utilities, and wholesale businesses, earnings usually are higher; in finance, insurance, real estate, and other types of office services, earnings generally are lower. Those working for large companies or national chains may receive excellent benefits. After one year of employment, some stock clerks are offered one to two weeks of paid vacation each year, as well as health and medical insurance and a retirement plan.

WORK ENVIRONMENT

Stock clerks usually work in relatively clean, comfortable areas. Working conditions vary considerably, however, depending on the industry and type of merchandise being handled. For example, stock clerks who handle refrigerated goods must spend some time in cold storage rooms, while those who handle construction materials, such as bricks and lumber, occasionally work outside in harsh weather. Most stock clerk jobs involve much standing, bending, walking, stretching, lifting, and carrying. Some workers may be required to operate machinery to lift and move stock.

Because stock clerks are employed in so many different types of industries, the amount of hours worked every week depends on the type of employer. Stock clerks in retail stores usually work a five-day, 40-hour week, while those in industry work 44 hours, or five and one half days, a week. Many others are able to find part-time work. Overtime is common, especially when large shipments arrive or during peak times such as holiday seasons.

OUTLOOK

Although the volume of inventory transactions is expected to increase significantly, employment for stock clerks is expected to decline through 2012, according to the U.S. Department of Labor. This is a result of increased automation and other productivity improvements that enable clerks to handle more stock. Manufacturing and wholesale trade industries are making the greatest use of automation. In addition to computerized inventory control systems, firms in these industries are expected to rely more on sophisticated conveyor belts, automatic high stackers to store and retrieve goods, and automatic guided vehicles that are battery-powered and driverless. Sales-floor stock clerks in grocery stores and department stores will probably be less affected by automation as most of their work is difficult to automate.

Because this occupation employs a large number of workers, many job openings will occur each year to replace stock clerks who transfer to other jobs and leave the labor force. Stock clerk jobs tend to be entry-level positions, so many vacancies will be created by normal career progression to other occupations.

FOR MORE INFORMATION

For materials on educational programs in the retail industry, contact
National Retail Federation
325 7th Street, NW, Suite 1100
Washington, DC 20004
http://www.nrf.com

Temporary Workers

QUICK FACTS

School Subjects
English
Speech

Personal Skills
Communication/ideas
Following instructions

Work Environment
Primarily indoors
Primary one location (per assignment)

Minimum Education Level
High school diploma

Salary Range
$10 to $25 to $50 an hour

Certification or Licensing
Required for certain positions

Outlook
Much faster than the average

DOT
N/A

GOE
N/A

NOC
N/A

O*NET-SOC
N/A

OVERVIEW

Employees who work on an assignment or contractual basis are called *temporary workers*. They usually work through agencies, staffing offices, or placement centers that place qualified workers in jobs lasting from one day to months according to their educational background, work experience, or profession.

People work as temps for several reasons. The majority of people temp because they are between full-time positions. Some enjoy the flexibility that temporary assignments offer. Others use the opportunity to try out different occupations or companies in hopes of being hired in a permanent capacity. Companies from almost every industry hire temporary workers to fill in when regular staff members are ill or on vacation. Special projects and seasonal work are other reasons for employment.

This is a vast industry, employing 2 million people per day in the United States, according to the American Staffing Association, which monitors the industry and represents about 1,600 agencies nationwide.

HISTORY

Throughout time, some people earned at least part of their income taking short jobs when the work was available. People even traveled to other towns for work, leaving their families behind. The National Association of Personnel Services records the earliest private employment services existed in 14th-century Germany, though no detail is available regarding the type of work. Kelly Services Inc. was one of the first temporary staffing agencies in the United States. In 1946 its founder, William Russell Kelly, realized there was a great demand for office and clerical help in Detroit, Michigan. Businesses throughout town needed reliable help, though not on a daily basis. Kelly's first employees were housewives and students—two groups with very flexible schedules. They were able to accept or decline assignments as their schedules allowed.

Soon other temporary agencies were placing qualified workers in a variety of businesses. The first temps were mainly receptionists or clerical help; many had no skills other than those associated with secretarial work. Temporary workers are better prepared today—most are computer savvy and have solid work experience. Also, a large number of temps are professionals with backgrounds in law, accounting, or health care, and there is a growing trend for placement agencies to focus on one specific occupational group.

THE JOB

The largest category of temporary workers is *administrative and clerical workers*, comprising almost half of all temporary workers in the United States. Reception, secretarial, and administrative work are some assignments in this category. In the past, collating, answering phones, typing, and filing were the major duties of temporary workers. Today, many administrative temporaries are skilled in word processing, various computer programs, and other procedures. Other administrative workers, such as medical secretaries, legal secretaries, and bookkeepers, have additional training and skills to help them better perform special duties.

Industrial workers are also employed as temporaries. Assignments may include inspecting, labeling, packaging, and record keeping in factories, warehouses, and docks. Staff shortages or seasonal peak periods are some reasons for contracting temporary help. Though a majority of industrial assignments do not require advanced training or skills, most businesses prefer temporaries to have past work experience.

Managerial temporaries come from a variety of backgrounds. This group includes retired businesspeople, recent M.B.A. graduates, and freelance business consultants. Many businesses hire managerial temporaries for short-term projects. For example, consultants may analyze a company's performance record, suggest and implement changes, and exit the project soon afterward. They are also hired to motivate staff or to expedite the release of a product or service. Temporaries hired in this field usually have degrees in business or related subjects; some have advanced degrees. Managerial temporaries with solid work experience or reputable references are highly desired.

Computer programmers, systems analysts, and *hardware and software engineers* are just some of the *information technology (IT) specialists* that work as temporaries. Often referred to as "techsperts," they are contracted to help meet deadlines or work on short-term projects. Companies find it more cost effective to hire temporary IT people than to train existing employees on the latest computer technology, especially when deadlines are short. *Web designers* are also in demand to design and create new company websites or tweak existing ones. *Help-desk specialists* are often enlisted to provide support for a company's IT department.

Professional occupations also provide abundant opportunities for those interested in short-term assignments. In recent years, companies have increasingly relied on contracting *accounting professionals* to compile financial reports, perform audits, and prepare company tax reports. Installing new accounting systems and training permanent staff in the use of such systems are other tasks completed by accounting temporaries. Businesses often hire temporaries to work on short-term projects or during seasonal peak periods. Smaller businesses, especially, rely on temporaries to provide manpower to their accounting departments. Accounting temps must have a degree in accounting, taxation, or business administration; many are certified public accountants.

Engineers or *scientists* are often hired to work on special projects or new research. Companies contract engineers to design and develop a new product from start to finish or a portion of the manufacturing process. Pharmaceutical companies need scientists of varying specialties to research, test, and develop new medicines. Temporary workers in this field are highly specialized. All are college graduates; most have advanced degrees and work experience in their specialties.

For special projects or to provide assistance in complicated legal cases, law firms often contract *lawyers* on a short-term basis to work alongside their existing legal team. Lawyers may be assigned to write and file briefs, take depositions, prepare witnesses for trial, or provide litigation support. *Paralegals* may also work on temporary assignments to research cases, prepare documents, or provide other legal assistance.

Health professionals are enjoying great growth in temporary services. *Nurses,* especially, are high in demand. Agencies are actively recruiting nurses for assignments ranging in length from one day to months at a time. Hospitals and nursing homes are often short staffed and rely on *registered nurses, licensed practical nurses,* and *certified nursing attendants* to work the less desirable night and weekend shifts. Health professionals may also be assigned to care for home health patients. Hospitals in rural towns or remote locations rely heavily on health professionals to work short-term contracts. *Physical therapists, radiological technicians, dialysis technicians, medical assistants,* and *medical records clerks* may also work on temporary assignments.

REQUIREMENTS

High School

Very few students plan their high school curriculum based on the goal of working as a temporary. Most people follow a chosen career path and find along the way that temporary work suits their personal lives, educational goals, or professional ambitions better than a full-time, long-term position.

High school courses in business, word processing, computers, math, and English will prepare you to work as an administrative or clerical temp. Otherwise, you should study the subjects that fit with your chosen career field.

Postsecondary Training

To work as a temp in any professional capacity, such as nursing, accounting, law, or information technology, you must complete the educational requirements for that profession and have some work experience. Many clients require temporary workers to have college degrees or solid training before offering non-entry-level assignments such as managerial or technical projects. Good computer and communication skills are a must.

For students with some postsecondary training, working as a temporary in an entry-level position can provide paid work experience and contacts that may help in later job searches.

Certification or Licensing

Certification or licensing is required for some professional temporary work. For example, before accepting a contract as a traveling nurse, you must have a license to practice in the state or country where the assignment is located. Likewise, lawyers must have a valid license to practice in the assigned location. Agencies will usually help temporary candidates apply for additional licenses or seek reciprocity.

Other Requirements

The transient nature of temporary work is not for everyone. Imagine having to adapt to a different set of coworkers with each assignment, not to mention a new office environment and the politics that go with it. For nurses and other medical workers on temporary or agency assignments, it means having to work your shift without the benefit of a hospital orientation. "You really need to be assertive" to succeed in this type of work environment, attests Mary Ann Mason, a nurse in Illinois. She prefers this type of working situation, since it gives her the flexibility to structure her workload around family activities.

EXPLORING

One of the major appeals of temporary work is the great flexibility and variety that it provides. Because almost every industry employs temporary workers, your options for exploring the field are vast. You can apply for a summer job or seasonal work during holidays. Usually, businesses look for extra help during busy times. Visit a temporary placement office and shadow a recruiter for the day. You'll see firsthand what recruiters look for when interviewing potential temporary workers. Do they have the proper skills and work experience? Do they look and act professional?

There are many websites devoted to the world of temporary work. Read personal work experiences, advice columns on how to survive new office politics, and tips on interviewing. See *The Contract Employee's Handbook* (http://www.cehandbook.com) or the Administrative Resource Network (http://www.adresnet.com).

EMPLOYERS

One of the greatest advantages of temporary work is that employment opportunities exist nationwide. Most temporary workers use an employment agency or staffing service to find assignments. If basic office skills are your strength, try agencies such as Kelly or Manpower Services. Both are known in the business world for having pools of dependable office support workers as well as highly trained professionals such as technical workers and engineers.

If you specialize in a certain profession, contact agencies that cater to those fields. Accountemps, based in California, for example, assigns certified public accountants and other accounting professionals to work on short-term and long-term projects throughout the United States, as well as in Europe and Australia. Special Counsel Incorporated, a nationwide legal staffing agency, places lawyers, paralegals, and legal assistants in temporary assignments. Clients include top law firms needing extra manpower for large projects, or corporations needing legal expertise.

STARTING OUT

Most temps work through an agency or placement center. Before the agency can place you, they will conduct a screening interview to assess your skills and work experience. You will need an updated resume, any certification or licensing papers, and a list of references. Be prepared to let the agency know of any preferences you may have in terms of assignments—type of project, location, hours, and any physical accommodations you may need. You may have to take several tests depending on the type of temp work for which you are applying. For example, administrative workers may have to take a test to measure their keyboarding speed or computer knowledge. Training is sometimes encouraged to keep temps current with computer programs and systems as demanded by clients. The agency may make security or professional checks, verify school transcripts, or order drug testing before you are given an assignment.

You can find a list of agencies and placement centers in your local phone book or on the Internet. Listings and ad will usually specify their specialties.

ADVANCEMENT

Many people view temporary work assignments as a great way to develop industry contacts. Solid work performance may catch the attention of management and result in a temp-to-hire situation. A temporary worker may also view advancement in terms of choice assignments with good companies offering higher pay.

Most agencies offer additional training, at no cost, to their employees. According to a survey conducted by the National Association of Temporary and Staffing Services, 66 percent of temporary workers acquire new skills while on assignments. As temporary workers gain knowledge with new equipment and software programs and acquire other highly desirable skills, they can progress to different temporary jobs, many with a better pay scale.

EARNINGS

Temporary workers are paid hourly or per project by the agency or personnel supply firm. In turn the agency bills the client company for every hour of work, including any fees or commission. According to the National Association of Temporary and Staffing Services, temps receive a little more than 70 percent of the billable rate; the agency keeps the remainder. For example, if the temp is paid $21 an hour, the agency actually bills the client $30 per hour and keeps the remaining

$9 as its commission. A 30 percent commission may seem high, but from this amount, the agency needs to pay the temp's Social Security, any training costs, job counseling, and office operating costs.

The hourly rate varies greatly depending on the type of work or occupation. Administrative workers make about $10 an hour or more, according to the American Staffing Association. On the higher end, some agencies offer $50 an hour or more for contract nurses. In addition, a stipend is offered to cover expenses such as travel and housing. This is often the case when the nurse or other health professional is assigned outside of their home base.

The *Occupational Outlook Handbook* reports that median hourly wages for temporary workers in 2003 ranged from $7.65 an hour for hand packers and packagers to $10.05 for receptionists and information clerks to $26.91 an hour for registered nurses.

For most kinds of temporary work, the hourly rate is much higher than that offered to permanent employees. This is possible because benefits such as paid vacation, sick time, health insurance, and other perks are not usually offered to temporary workers. Some agencies may offer benefits to temporary workers after they log in a specific number of working days. Benefits may include medical coverage and short-term disability insurance, but the employee contribution for such benefits is usually higher compared to the contribution paid by full-time, permanent workers. Many temps receive insurance benefits from other sources, most often a spouse working in a full-time job.

WORK ENVIRONMENT

The work environment depends on the particular assignment. Industrial work most often takes place at factories or outdoor facilities. Most office assignments are indoors. Some agencies ask clients to provide temporary workers with desks or designated workspaces, especially if the project is long-term.

Workdays and hours also vary from assignment to assignment. Usually temporary workers follow the company's work hours. However, if a project deadline is looming, temporary workers may be asked to work overtime or on weekends.

Temporary workers are not usually given preferential treatment by their clients. Work spaces may be small, and interaction with permanent staff, both on professional and social levels, may be limited. Projects are likely to be the ones no one else wants to do. Support staff temporaries, especially, may be faced with mountains of papers to collate, staple, and hand out, while simultaneously answering a bank of phones. On the other hand, some offices may view temporary workers as much needed and appreciated manpower to meet tough deadlines.

OUTLOOK

Because almost every industry—from manufacturing to health care—uses temporary workers or consultants, employment opportunities abound. In fact, according to the *Occupational Outlook Handbook,* this field is expected to grow much faster than the average. This industry is expected to add almost 1.8 million new jobs during the 2002–12 period, making temporary employment one of the fastest growing industries in the United States. Most new jobs will occur in the largest occupational groups: office and administrative support, production, and transportation and material moving. There will also be many opportunities in specialized fields such as nursing, health care, accounting, and information technology.

In order to stay competitive, companies must be cost effective. Temporary workers can give companies the power of additional manpower to meet important deadlines or work on special projects and provide support when they are short staffed. Contracting temps saves businesses money because they do not have to pay costly benefits for temporary staff. Also, companies can save time by contracting with temps already trained in a particular computer program instead of retraining existing employees. The American Staffing Association expects that temps in professional occupations, especially health care, law, and engineering, will be in great demand. Many new jobs will occur in federal, state, and local governments that will continue to contract many of its projects.

Many people enjoy working in a temporary work environment because it allows them the flexibility of choosing when and where to work. Others take advantage of temp work because it gives them access to free training. People who are unsure of their career path view temp work as a chance to audition different industries before committing to one. However, a majority of temporary workers are between jobs or are using their temporary assignments as a possible bridge to full-time employment.

While flexibility is a major perk associated with temporary work, it can also be a serious disadvantage. Once an assignment is complete, temporary workers are usually the first to be let go during a slow economy. Given a smaller working budget, businesses tend to manage with existing employees instead of contracting additional help. Also, the notion of hiring temporary workers when a company is downsizing its workforce is considered bad office politics.

FOR MORE INFORMATION

For industry information and trends, contact
American Staffing Association
277 South Washington Street, Suite 200
Alexandria, VA 22314
Tel: 703-253-2020
Email: asa@staffingtoday.net
http://www.staffingtoday.net

National Association of Personnel Services
10905 Fort Washington Road, Suite 400
Fort Washington, MD 20744
Tel: 301-203-6700
http://www.napsweb.org

For temporary employment in the accounting industry, contact
Accountemps
http://www.accountemps.com

For general temporary employment opportunities, contact
Manpower
http://www.manpower.com

Kelly Services
http://www.kellyservices.com

For information on temporary employment opportunities in the law industry, contact
Special Counsel
1 Independent Drive
Jacksonville, FL 32202
Tel: 800-737-3436
Email: info@specialcounsel.com
http://www.specialcounsel.com

Typists and Word Processors

OVERVIEW

Using typewriters, personal computers, and other office machines, *typists* and *word processors* convert handwritten or otherwise unfinished material into clean, readable, typewritten copies. Typists create reports, letters, forms, tables, charts, and other materials for all kinds of businesses and services. Word processors create the same types of materials using a computer that stores information electronically instead of printing it directly onto paper. Other typists use special machines that convert manuscripts into Braille, coded copy, or typeset copy. Typists and word processors hold about 241,000 jobs in the United States.

HISTORY

The invention of the typewriter in 1829 by W. A. Burt greatly increased business efficiency and productivity, and its benefits grew as typists became skilled at quickly transforming messy handwritten documents into neat, consistently typed copies.

More recently, the introduction of word processing into the workplace has revolutionized typing. This task may be done on a personal computer, a computer terminal hooked up to a network, or a computer that strictly handles word processing functions. By typing documents on a computer screen, workers can correct errors and make any necessary changes before a hard copy is printed, thus eliminating the need for retyping whole pages to correct mistakes. The computer stores the information in its memory, so the worker can go back to it again and again for copies or changes.

Some typists and word processors telecommute from their homes.
(Getty Images)

The term *word processing* entered the English language in 1965, when International Business Machines, more commonly known as IBM, introduced a typewriter that put information onto magnetic tape instead of paper. Corrections could be made on this tape before running the tape through a machine that converted the signals on the tape into characters on a printed page. Today, word processing software and personal computers have virtually replaced typewriters in the office.

THE JOB

Some typists perform few duties other than typing. These workers spend approximately 75 percent of their time at the keyboard. They may input statistical data, medical reports, legal briefs, addresses, letters, and other documents from handwritten copies. They may work in pools, dividing the work of a large office among many workers under the supervision of a typing section chief. These typists may also be responsible for making photocopies of typewritten materials for distribution.

Beginning typists may start by typing address labels, headings on form letters, and documents from legible handwritten copy. More experienced typists may work from copy that is more difficult to read and requires the use of independent judgement when typing; they may be responsible for typing complex statistical tables, for example.

Clerk-typists spend up to 50 percent of their time typing. They also perform a variety of clerical tasks such as filing, answering the phone, acting as receptionists, and operating copy machines.

Many typists type from recorded audiotapes instead of written or printed copy. *Transcribing-machine operators* sit at keyboards and wear headsets, through which they hear the spoken contents of letters, reports, and meetings. Typists can control the speed of the tape so they can comfortably type every word they hear. They proofread their finished documents and may erase dictated tapes for future reuse.

Almost all typists work at computer terminals. *Magnetic-tape typewriter operators* enter information from written materials on computers to produce magnetic disks or tapes for storage and later retrieval. *In-file operators* use terminals to post or receive information about people's credit records for credit reporting agencies. When an agency subscriber calls with a question about a person's credit, the typist calls up that record on the video display terminal screen and reads the information.

Most typists today are *word processors*. These employees put documents into the proper format by entering codes into the word processing software, telling it which lines to center, which words to underline, where the margins should be set, and how the document should be stored and printed. Word processors can edit, change, insert, and delete materials instantly just by pressing keys. Word processing is particularly efficient for form letters, in which only certain parts of a document change on each copy. When a word processor has finished formatting and keying in a document, the document is sent electronically to a printer for a finished copy. The document is normally saved on a disk or the computer's hard drive so that any subsequent changes to it can be made easily and new copies produced immediately. Word processors also can send electronic files via email or modems to people in different locations.

Certain typists use special machines to create copy. *Perforator typists* type on machines that punch holes in a paper tape, which is used to create typewritten copy automatically. In publishing and printing, *photocomposing-perforator machine operators, photocomposing-keyboard operators, veritype operators,* and *typesetter-perforator operators* type on special machines that produce photographic negatives or paper prints of the copy. Some of these typists must also code copy to show what size and style of letters and characters should be used and how the layout of the page should look.

Braille typists and *Braille operators* use special typewriter-like machines to transcribe written or spoken English into Braille. By pressing one key or a combination of keys, they create the raised characters of the Braille alphabet. They may print either on special paper or on metal plates, which are later used to print books or other publications.

Cryptographic machine operators operate typewriter-like equipment that codes, transmits, and decodes secret messages for the armed forces, law enforcement agencies, and business organizations. These typists select a code card from a codebook, insert the card into the machine, and type the message in English on the machine, which converts it to coded copy. A decoding card is used to follow the same process for decoding.

REQUIREMENTS

High School

Most employers require that typists and word processors be high school graduates and able to type accurately at a rate of at least 40–50 words per minute. Typists need a good knowledge of spelling, grammar, and punctuation and may be required to be familiar with standard office equipment.

Postsecondary Training

You can learn typing and word processing skills through courses offered by colleges, business schools, and home-study programs.

Some people learn keyboarding through self-teaching materials such as books or computer programs. Business schools and community colleges often offer certificates or associate's degrees for typists and word processors.

For those who do not pursue such formal education, temporary agencies will often train workers in these skills. Generally, it takes a minimum of three to six months of experience to become a skilled word processor.

Word processors must be able to type 45 to 80 words per minute and should know the proper way to organize such documents as letters, reports, and financial statements. Increasingly, employers are requiring that employees know how to use various software programs for word processing, spreadsheet, and database management tasks.

Other Requirements

To be a successful typists and word processor, you need manual dexterity and the ability to concentrate. You should be alert, efficient, and attentive to detail. Because you will often work directly with other people, you need good interpersonal skills, including a courteous and cheerful demeanor. Good listening skills are important in order to transcribe recorded material.

EXPLORING

As with many clerical occupations, a good way to gain experience as a typist is through high school work-study programs. Students in these programs work part time for local businesses and attend classes part time. Temporary agencies also provide training and temporary jobs for exploring the field. Another way to gain typing experience is to volunteer to type for friends, church groups, or other organizations and to create your own computerized reports.

EMPLOYERS

Typists and word processors are employed in almost every kind of workplace, including banks, law firms, factories, schools, hospitals, publishing firms, department stores, and government agencies. They may work with groups of employees in large offices or with only one or two other people in small offices.

There are approximately 241,000 are word processors and typists working in the United States. Most of these workers are employed by firms that provide business services, including temporary help, word processing, and computer and data processing. Many also work for federal, state, and local government agencies. Some typists and word processors telecommute, working on client projects from their own home offices.

STARTING OUT

Business school and college students may learn of typing or word processing positions through their schools' placement offices. Some large businesses recruit employees directly from these schools. High school guidance counselors also may know of local job openings.

People interested in typing or word processor positions can check the want ads in newspapers and business journals for companies with job openings. They can apply directly to the personnel departments of large companies that hire many of these workers. They also can register with temporary agencies. To apply for positions with the federal government, job seekers should apply at the nearest regional Office of Personnel Management. State, county, and city governments may also have listings for such positions.

ADVANCEMENT

Typists and word processors usually receive salary increases as they gain experience and are promoted from junior to senior positions. These are often given a classification or pay scale designation, such as typist or word processor I or II. They may also advance from clerk-typist to technical typist, or from a job in a typing pool to a typing position in a private office.

A degree in business management or executive secretarial skills increases a typist's chances for advancement. In addition, many large companies and government agencies provide training programs that allow workers to upgrade their skills and move into other jobs, such as secretary, statistical clerk, or stenographer.

Once they have acquired enough experience, some typists and word processors go into business for themselves by working from home and providing typing services to business clients. They may find work typing reports, manuscripts, and papers for professors, authors, business people, and students.

The more word processing experience an employee has, the better the opportunities to move up. Some may be promoted to word processing supervisor or selected for in-house professional training programs in data processing. Word processors may also move into related fields and work as word-processing equipment salespeople or servicers or word-processing teachers or consultants.

EARNINGS

The U.S. Department of Labor reports that median annual earnings of word processors and typists in 2002 were $26,730. Salaries ranged from less than $17,750 to more than $40,450. Word processors and typists employed by local governments made the highest median annual salaries in 2002: $27,840.

Typists and word processors occasionally may work overtime to finish special projects and may receive overtime pay. In large cities workers usually receive paid holidays, two weeks' vacation after one year of employment, sick leave, health and life insurance, and a pension plan. Some large companies also provide dental insurance, profit sharing opportunities, and bonuses.

WORK ENVIRONMENT

Typists and word processors usually work 35–40 hours per week at workstations in clean, bright offices. They usually sit most of the day in a fairly small area. The work is detailed and often repetitious, and approaching deadlines may increase the pressure and demands placed on typists and word processors.

Recent years have seen a controversy develop concerning the effect that working at video display terminals (VDTs) can have on workers' health. Working with these screens in improper lighting can cause eyestrain, and sitting at a workstation all day can cause musculoskeletal stress and pain. The computer industry is paying closer attention to these problems and is working to improve health and safety standards in VDT-equipped offices.

Another common ailment for typists and word processors is carpal tunnel syndrome, a painful ailment of the tendons in the wrist that is triggered by repetitive movement. If left unchecked, it can require corrective surgery. However, proper placement of the typing keyboard can help prevent injury. Several companies have designed desks, chairs, and working spaces that accommodate the physical needs of typists and word processors in the best manner currently known.

The nature of this work lends itself to flexible work arrangements. Many typists and word processors work in temporary positions that provide flexible schedules. About 20 percent work part time. Some offices allow word processors and typists to telecommute from home, whereby they receive and send work on home computers via modems. These jobs may be especially convenient for workers with disabilities or family responsibilities, but often they do not provide a full range of benefits and lack the advantages of social interaction on the job.

OUTLOOK

Employment in the typing field is expected to decline through 2012 due to the increasing automation of offices. Technological innovations such as scanners, voice-recognition software, and electronic data transmission are being used in more workplaces, reducing the need for typists and word processors. Many office workers now do their own word processing because word processing and data entry software has become so user-friendly. However, the sheer size of the occupation means that many jobs will become available for typists and word processors, especially to replace those employees who change careers or leave the workforce.

More companies today are contracting out their data entry and word processing projects to temporary-help and staffing services firms. Most openings will be with these types of firms, and jobs will go to workers who have the best technical skills and knowledge of several word processing programs.

FOR MORE INFORMATION

For industry information, contact the IAAP.

International Association of Administrative Professionals (IAAP)
10502 NW Ambassador Drive
PO Box 20404
Kansas City, MO 64195
Tel: 816-891-6600
Email: service@iaap-hq.org
http://www.iaap-hq.org

Index

Entries and page numbers in **bold** indicate major treatment of a topic.

A

accountants and auditors 4–16
accredited business accountant (ABA) 8
accredited tax advisor (ATA) 8
accredited tax preparer (ATP) 8
advancement 10
assurance accountants 6
bank examiners 5
budget accountants 6
certification 8–9
certified information systems auditor (CISA) 8
certified internal auditor (CIA) 8
certified management accountants (CMAs) 8
certified public accountants (CPAs) 8, 10
chief bank examiners 7
cost accountants 6
earnings 10–11
employers 9
environmental accountants 6
exploring field 9
forensic accountants and auditors 6
general accountants 5–6
government accountants 5
high school requirements 7
history 4–5
industrial accountants 5
information 13–14
internal auditors 6–7
Internal Revenue Service agents 5
interview 14–16
investigators 5
job, described 5–7
licensing 8–9
management accountants 5
outlook 11–12
postsecondary training 7–8
private accountants 5
property accountants 6
public accountants 5
requirements 7–9
revenue agents 7
starting out 9–10
systems accountants 6
tax accountants 6
tax auditors 7
work environment 11
account information clerks 25
accounting clerks. *See* bookkeeping and accounting clerks
accounting professionals 166
accredited business accountant (ABA) 8
accredited purchasing practitioner (APP) 135
accredited tax advisor (ATA) 8
accredited tax preparer (ATP) 8
administrative and clerical workers 165
administrative assistants 148–156
administrative clerks 105
Administrative Resource Network 168
administrative secretaries 149
Affina 48–49, 52
affirmative-action coordinators 113
AFL-CIO 81–82
agricultural accountants 4
American Council for Accountancy and Taxation 8
American Federation of Labor (AFL) 81
American Federation of State, County, and Municipal Employees 26
American Field Service International (AFS) 44
American Institute of Certified Public Accountants (AICPA) 8, 9
American Management Association Self-Study Certificate Program 99
American Purchasing Society 133, 135
American Staffing Association 164, 170, 171
answering-service operators 143
area managers 32
assistant buyers 138
associates
executive recruiters 75
management analysts and consultants 93
Association of Executive Search Consultants (AESC) 79
assurance accountants 6
audit clerks 24–25
auditors. *See* accountants and auditors
automobile club information clerks 143

B

Bank Administration Institute 9
Bell, Alexander Graham 48
benefits managers 115
billing and rate clerks 25
billing clerks 17–22
advancement 20–21
billing-machine operators 19
COD (cash-on-delivery) clerks 19
deposit-refund clerks 19
earnings 21
employers 20
exploring field 20
foreign clerks 19
high school requirements 19
history 17–18
information 22
interline clerks 19
invoice-control clerks 19
job, described 18–19
outlook 21–22
passenger rate clerks 19
postsecondary training 19
rate reviewers 19
raters 19
requirements 19–20
service clerks 19

settlement clerks 19
starting out 20
telegraph-service clerks 19
work environment 21
billing-machine operators 19
bookkeeping and accounting clerks 23–28
account information clerks 25
advancement 27
audit clerks 24–25
billing and rate clerks 25
earnings 27
employers 26
exploring field 26
fixed-capital clerks 25
general bookkeepers 24
general-ledger bookkeepers 24
high school requirements 25
history 23–24
information 28
job, described 24–25
outlook 28
postsecondary training 25
requirements 25–26
starting out 26–27
work environment 27–28
Bowe, Jeff 31, 33, 35–36
Braille operators 176
Braille typists 176
budget accountants 6
Bureau of Labor Statistics 38, 94, 101, 121, 130
Burt, W. A. 173
Bush, George W. 47
business managers 29–39
advancement 36
area managers 32
chief financial officers (CFO) 32
chief operating officers (COO) 31
district managers 32
earnings 36–37
employers 35
executive vice presidents 31–32
exploring field 34–35
high school requirements 32–33
history 29–30
information 38–39
job, described 30–32
magazines for managers 34
outlook 37–38
postsecondary training 33
president 31
regional managers 32
requirements 32–34
starting out 35–36
work environment 37

C
certified administrative professional (CAP) 152
certified information systems auditor (CISA) 8
certified internal auditor (CIA) 8
certified legal secretary specialist (CLSS) 152
certified management accountants (CMAs) 8

certified nursing attendants 167
certified professional public buyer (CPPB) 135
certified professional secretary (CPS) 152
certified public accountants (CPAs) 8, 10
certified public purchasing officer (CPPO) 135
certified purchasing manager (CPM) 135
chief financial officers (CFO) 32
chief operating officers (COO) 31
Clark, William 40
clerk-typists 175
closed shops 82
COD (cash-on-delivery) clerks 19
communications specialists 125–132
compensation analysts 114
compensation managers 114
Complete Guide for Occupational Exploration 2
computer programmers 166
conciliators 83
concrete products dispatchers 105
conference managers 64–65
congressional-district aides 105
Congress of Industrial Organizations (CIO) 82
consultants. *See also* management analysts and consultants
executive recruiters 75
contingency recruiters 74
The Contract Employee's Handbook 168
convention managers 64–65
coordinators of auxiliary personnel 115
cost accountants 6
Cox, Julie 48–53
craft unions 82, 83
Crane Federal Credit Union 113
cryptographic machine operators 176
cultural advisers 40–46
advancement 45
earnings 45
employers 44
exploring field 43–44
high school requirements 43
history 40
information 46
job, described 41–43
memo, translation *42*
outlook 45
postsecondary training 43
requirements 43
starting out 44–45
words to learn 41
work environment 45
customer care representatives 47–55
customer service representatives 47–55
advancement 52–53
certification 50
earnings 53
employers 52
exploring field 51–52
high school requirements 50
history 47–48
information 54–55
job, described 48–50

licensing 50
outlook 53–54
perfection, working for 51
postsecondary training 50
requirements 50–51
starting out 52
work environment 53
Customer Service Week 47
cut-file clerks 160

D

data-coder operators 58
data entry clerks 56–62
advancement 60
data-coder operators 58
data typists 58
earnings 60–61
employers 60
exploring field 59–60
high school requirements 59
history 56–57
information 62
job, described 57–59
keypunch operators 58
outlook 61–62
postsecondary training 59
requirements 59
service operators 58
starting out 60
terminal operators 58–59
verifier operators 58
work environment 61
data typists 58
Department of Defense 93
deposit-refund clerks 19
dialysis technicians 167
Dictionary of Occupational Titles (DOT) 2
"differential piecework" plan 89–90
directors
management analysts and consultants 94
public relations 127
Directory of Executive Recruiters ("Red
Book") 78
Disc Graphics 31
district managers 32

E

Eckerle, Susan 112–113, 117, 120
education and training manager 114
education secretaries 150
EEO representatives 113
"efficiency cult" 89
EmCare Inc. 122
employee-health maintenance program specialists 115
employee-welfare managers 115
employer relations representatives 115
employment interviewers 113
employment managers 113
Employment Retirement Security Act (ERISA)
115
*Encyclopedia of Careers and Vocational
Guidance* 1

engagement managers 93
engineers 166
ENIAC (computer) 56
environmental accountants 6
equal employment opportunity (EEO)
113–114
ethics in recruiting 75
event planners 63–72
advancement 68–69
certification 66
conference managers 64–65
convention managers 64–65
earnings 69
employers 67–68
exploring field 67
high school requirements 66
history 63–64
information 70
interview 70–72
job, described 64–66
licensing 66
outlook 69–70
party planners 65–66
postsecondary training 66
requirements 66–67
special-event coordinators 65
starting out 68
trade show managers 64–65
work environment 69
executive recruiters 73–80
advancement 78
associates 75
certification 76
consultants 75
contingency recruiters 74
earnings 78–79
employers 78
ethics in recruiting 75
exploring field 77–78
high school requirements 76
history 73–74
information 80
job, described 74–76
licensing 76
outlook 79–80
postsecondary training 76
requirements 76–77
researchers 74
retainer recruiters 73–74
starting out 78
work environment 79
executive vice presidents 31–32

F

Federal Arbitration Act 112
Felix, Peter 79–80
field contractors 134
file clerks 105
fixed-capital clerks 25
foreign clerks 19
forensic accountants and
auditors 6
fund-raising directors 127

G

general accountants 5–6
general bookkeepers 24
general-ledger bookkeepers 24
government accountants 5
government personnel specialists 116–117
grain broker-and-market operators 134
grain buyers 134
Gregg, John Robert 148
Guerrera, Claudio 14–16
Guide for Occupational Exploration (GOE) 2

H

hardware and software engineers 166
head of purchasing 138
head tobacco buyers 134
health professionals 166–167
help-desk specialists 166
hosts and hostesses 141
Human Resources Development Canada 2
human resources professionals 111–124

I

IBM (International Business Machines) 174–175
industrial accountants 5
industrial relations directors 113
industrial unions 82–83
industrial workers 165
in-file operators 143, 175
information clerks 141–147
Information Systems Audit and Control Association 8
information technology (IT) specialists 166
Institute for Supply Management 133, 135
Institute of Management Consultants 92
interline clerks 19
internal auditors 6–7
International Association for Exhibition Management 66
International Association of Administrative Professionals 151, 152
International Association of Business Communicators 128
The International Association of Corporate and Professional Recruiters 77
International Customer Service Association 47, 50, 51
International Foundation of Employee Benefits 118
International Union of Electronics, Electrical, Salaries, Machine, and Furniture Workers 26
Internet 48, 54, 169
interviews
    accountants and auditors 14–16
    event planners 70–72
    personnel and labor relations specialists 122–124
inventory clerks 158
invoice-control clerks 19

J

JIST Works 2
job analysts 114
job development specialists 113
Jones, Renee 122–124
Junior Achievement 93
junior buyers 138
junior partners 94

K

Kelly Services Inc. 164–165, 168
Kelly, William Russell 165
keypunch operators 58
kitchen clerks 160

L

labor relations specialists. *See* personnel and labor relations specialists
labor union business agents 81–88
    advancement 85–86
    conciliators 83
    earnings 86
    employers 85
    exploring field 85
    high school requirements 84
    history 81–82
    information 87–88
    job, described 82–84
    mediators 83
    outlook 86–87
    postsecondary training 84
    referees 83
    requirements 84
    shop stewards 83
    starting out 85
    umpires 83
    work environment 86
lawyers 166
Lee, Ivy Ledbetter 125
legal secretaries 150, 152
Lewis, Meriwether 40
licensed practical nurses 166
linen room attendants 160
lobbyists 127

M

magazine keepers 160
magazines for managers 34
magnetic-tape typewriter operators 175
management accountants 5
management analysts and consultants 89–96
    advancement 93–94
    associate 93
    certification 92
    directors 94
    earnings 94
    employers 93
    engagement managers 93
    exploring field 92–93
    high school requirements 91
    history 89–90
    information 95–96

job, described 90–91
junior partners 94
licensing 92
outlook 95
partners 94
postsecondary training 91–92
principals 94
requirements 91–92
senior associate 93
senior engagement managers 93–94
starting out 93
work environment 94–95
managerial temporaries 165–166
Manpower Services 168
Mason, Mary Ann 168
material clerks 158
materials managers 138
McKinsey, James O. 90
media specialists 125–132
mediators 83, 116
medical assistants 167
medical records clerks 167
medical secretaries 150
Meeting Professionals International 66, 69
Meetings & Conventions 67
membership secretaries 150
merchandise distributors 158
metal control coordinators 160
Midvale Steel plant 90

N
National Association of Colleges and
   Employers 120
National Association of Legal Secretaries 152
National Association of Personnel Services
   164
National Association of Purchasing Agents
   133
National Association of Temporary and
   Staffing Services 169
*National Directory of Occupational Titles
   and Codes* 63
National Institute of Government Purchasing
   135
National Labor Relations Board 82
New York Chamber of Commerce 112
New York Times 74
North American Free Trade Agreement 40

O
occupational analysts 114
Occupational Information Network (O*NET)
   2
Occupational Information Network
   (O*NET)-Standard Occupational
   Classification System (SOC) 2
Occupational Outlook Handbook 2, 94, 120,
   146, 170, 171
office administrators 97–103
   advancement 101
   earnings 101
   employers 100
   exploring field 100

high school requirements 99
history 97–98
information 102–103
job, described 98–99
outlook 102
postsecondary training 99
requirements 99–100
starting out 100–101
work environment 101–102
Office and Professional Employees
   International Union 26
office clerks 104–110
   administrative clerks 105
   advancement 108–109
   books to read 108
   concrete products dispatchers 105
   congressional-district aides 105
   earnings 109
   employers 106
   exploring field 106
   file clerks 105
   high school requirements 106
   history 104
   information 110
   job, described 105
   outlook 109
   police clerks 105
   postsecondary training 106
   requirements 106
   starting out 107–108
   work environment 109
Office of Personnel Management 60, 178
OfficeTeam 101, 145
2002 Salary Guide 60
order fillers 158
Orta, Miguel 44–45

P
Pacioli, Luca 4
paralegals 166
park aides 143
partners 94
parts clerks 160
parts order and stock clerks 160
party planners 65–66
passenger rate clerks 19
Pennsylvania, University of 56
perforator typists 176
personal secretaries 150
personnel and labor relations specialists
   111–124
   advancement 119–120
   affirmative-action coordinators 113
   benefits managers 115
   certification 118
   compensation analysts 114
   compensation managers 114
   coordinators of auxiliary personnel 115
   earnings 120
   education and training manager 114
   EEO representatives 113
   employee-health maintenance program
      specialists 115

employee-welfare managers 115
employer relations representatives 115
employers 119
employment interviewers 113
employment managers 113
exploring field 118–119
government personnel specialists 116–117
high school requirements 117
history 111–112
industrial relations directors 113
information 121–122
interview 122–124
job analysts 114
job, described 112–117
job development specialists 113
licensing 118
occupational analysts 114
outlook 121
personnel managers 113
postsecondary training 117–118
professional conciliators 116
professional mediators 116
requirements 117–118
retirement officers 115
starting out 119
training specialists 114–115
work environment 120
personnel managers 113
photocomposing-keyboard operators 176
photocomposing-perforator machine operator 176
physical therapists 167
Pitman, Isaac 148
police clerks 105
prescription clerks 160
president 31
principals 94
private accountants 5
professional conciliators 116
Professional Convention Management Association (PCMA) 69–70
professional mediators 116
property accountants 6
property custodians 160
public accountants 5
Public Relations Society of America 128
public relations specialists 125–132
advancement 129–130
certification 128
director of public relations 127
earnings 130
employers 129
exploring field 128–129
fund-raising directors 127
high school requirements 127
history 125–126
information 131–132
job, described 126–127
licensing 128
lobbyists 127
outlook 131
postsecondary training 127–128
requirements 127–128

starting out 129
work environment 130–131
purchasing agents 133–140
accredited purchasing practitioner (APP) 135
advancement 138
assistant buyers 138
books to read 136
certification 135
certified professional public buyer (CPPB) 135
certified public purchasing officer (CPPO) 135
certified purchasing manager (CPM) 135
earnings 138
employers 137
exploring field 136–137
field contractors 134
grain broker-and-market operators 134
grain buyers 134
head of purchasing 138
head tobacco buyers 134
high school requirements 135
history 133
information 139–140
job, described 134
junior buyers 138
licensing 135
materials managers 138
outlook 139
postsecondary training 135
purchasing directors 134, 138
purchasing managers 134
requirements 135–136
starting out 137
vice-president of purchasing 138
work environment 138–139
purchasing directors 134, 138
Purchasing magazine 137
purchasing managers 134

R
radiological technicians 167
"rank and file" 82
rate reviewers 19
raters 19
receptionists 141–147
advancement 145
answering-service operators 143
automobile club information clerks 143
earnings 145–146
employers 145
exploring field 144–145
high school requirements 143
history 141–142
in-file operators 143
job, described 142–143
outlook 146
park aides 143
postsecondary training 143–144
referral-and-information aides 143
registrars 143
requirements 143–144

starting out 145
tourist-information assistants 143
work environment 146
referees 83
referral-and-information aides 143
regional managers 32
registered nurses 166
registrars 143
researchers 74
retainer recruiters 73–74
retirement officers 115
Robert Half International 11

S

Sacajawea 40
scientists 166
secretaries 148–156
administrative secretaries 149
advancement 153
certification 152
earnings 154
education secretaries 150
employers 153
exploring field 152–153
high school requirements 151
history 148–149
information 155–156
job, described 149–151
legal secretaries 150, 152
licensing 152
medical secretaries 150
membership secretaries 150
outlook 154–155
personal secretaries 150
postsecondary training 151–152
requirements 151–152
skills for success 151
social secretaries 150
starting out 153
technical secretaries 150
work environment 154
senior associates 93
senior engagement managers 93–94
service clerks 19
service operators 58
settlement clerks 19
shipping and receiving clerks 158
shop stewards 83
Shoshone Indian tribe 40
social secretaries 150
space and storage clerks 160
Sparkman, Darrell 70–72
Special Counsel Incorporated 168
special-event coordinators 65
stock clerks 157–163
advancement 161–162
cut-file clerks 160
earnings 162
employers 161
exploring field 161
high school requirements 160
history 157
information 163

inventory clerks 158
job, described 157–160
kitchen clerks 160
linen room attendants 160
magazine keepers 160
material clerks 158
merchandise distributors 158
metal control coordinators 160
order fillers 158
outlook 163
parts clerks 160
parts order and stock clerks 160
prescription clerks 160
property custodians 160
requirements 160–161
shipping and receiving clerks 158
space and storage clerks 160
starting out 161
stock control clerks 158
tool crib attendants 159
work environment 162–163
stock control clerks 158
switchboard operators 141
systems accountants 6
systems analysts 166

T

Taft-Hartley Act 82
tax accountants 6
tax auditors 7
Taylor, Frederick W. 89–90
technical secretaries 150
telecommuting *174*
telegraph-service clerks 19
temporary workers 164–172
accounting professionals 166
administrative and clerical workers 165
advancement 169
certification 167
certified nursing attendants 167
computer programmers 166
dialysis technicians 167
earnings 169–170
employers 168
engineers 166
exploring field 168
hardware and software engineers 166
health professionals 166–167
help-desk specialists 166
high school requirements 167
history 164–165
industrial workers 165
information 172
information technology (IT) specialists 166
job, described 165–167
lawyers 166
licensed practical nurses 166
licensing 167
managerial temporaries 165–166
medical assistants 167
medical records clerks 167
outlook 171
paralegals 166

physical therapists 167
postsecondary training 167
radiological technicians 167
registered nurses 166
requirements 167–168
scientists 166
starting out 169
systems analysts 166
work environment 170–171
terminal operators 58–59
tool crib attendants 159
tourist-information assistants 143
trade show managers 64–65
training specialists 114–115
transcribing-machine operators 175
2002 Salary Guide 60
typesetting-perforator operators 176
typists and word processors 173–180
advancement 178
Braille operators 176
Braille typists 176
clerk-typists 175
cryptographic machine operators 176
earnings 179
employers 177–178
exploring field 177
high school requirements 176
history 173–175
in-file operators 175
information 180
job, described 175–176
magnetic-tape typewriter operators 175
outlook 180
perforator typists 176

photocomposing-keyboard operators 176
photocomposing-perforator machine operator 176
postsecondary training 176–177
requirements 176–177
starting out 178
telecommuting 174
transcribing-machine operators 175
typesetting-perforator operators 176
veritype operators 176
work environment 179

U
umpires 83
Uniform CPA Examination 8
union shops 82
UNIVAC (computer) 56
U.S. Department of Labor 2, 10, 12, 21, 27, 28, 37, 53, 61, 82, 87, 95, 109, 131, 138, 154, 162, 163, 179
U.S. News & World Report 79

V
verifier operators 58
veritype operators 176
vice-president of purchasing 138
video display terminals (VDTs) 179

W
Wagner Act 82
Wall Street Journal 74
Wedgwood, Josiah 89
word processors. See typists and word processors